CAREERS IN INTERNATIONAL LAW

The University
of **Law**

incorporating The College of Law

The University of Law, 2 Bunhill Row, London, EC1Y 8HQ
Telephone: 01483 216371 E-mail: library-moorgate@law.ac.uk

Birmingham ' Bristol ' Chester ' Guildford ' London ' Manchester ' York

Printed in the United States of America.

12 11 10 09 08 5 4 3 2

Library of Congress Cataloging-in-Publication Data

Careers in international law / edited by Salli Anne Swartz.—3rd ed.
    p. cm.
  Includes index.
  ISBN-13: 978-1-59031-948-2
  ISBN-10: 1-59031-948-6
  1. International law—Study and teaching. 2. International law—Vocational guidance. 3. International law—Vocational guidance—United States. 4. Lawyers, Foreign—Vocational guidance—United States. I. Swartz, Salli. II. American Bar Association. Section of International Law.

KZ1238.U55C37 2008
341.023—dc22

2007048741

Contents

Preface   xiii

About the Editor   xv

About the Contributors   xix

Profile of the ABA Section
    of International Law   xxvii

Part 1
Foreign Practice   *1*

Chapter 1
*Demystifying the Career of an International
Derivatives Lawyer*   *3*
by Jeffrey B. Golden

   A.   Introduction   3

   B.   Why Derivatives Are Relevant   6

   C.   What Are Derivatives?   7

   D.   Why Do You Do It?   8

   E.   What Does It Involve?   8

   F.   When Does It Get Interesting?   9

   G.   One Last Tip   9

Chapter 2
How Do You Get from Philadelphia to Paris?   11
by Salli A. Swartz

  A. Introduction   11

  B. The Beginnings   11

  C. The Struggle   12

  D. The Breakthrough   13

  E. Success Is Just Around the Corner   14

  F. The Jump to Independence   14

  G. How to Prepare for a Career in International Law   17

      1. *What Is International Law?*   *17*

      2. *In What Type of Environment Do I Want to Practice?*   *18*

      3. *What Are My Lifestyle Choices?*   *18*

  H. Lessons Learned   20

      1. *Compromises in Job Choices*   *20*

      2. *Manage Expectations*   *20*

      3. *Find Mentors and Join Associations*   *20*

      4. *Take What Comes Your Way and Use the Experience to Your Benefit*   *22*

      5. *Certain Truths Remain Constant*   *22*

      6. *Travel and Learn about Different Cultures and Languages*   *23*

  I. Conclusion   24

Chapter 3
What You Find Out After You Find Ice   25
by Bruce Horowitz

  A. Finding Ice   25

  B. Finding the Law   27

  C. Finding Peace   28

  D. Finding a Peaceful Place to Practice Law   29

  E. Finding Your Own Path   31

Chapter 4
My Career as a Latin-American Transactional Lawyer   33
by Andrew J. Markus

  A. Introduction   33

B. Why I Became an International Lawyer 34

C. Law Firm Practice 34

D. What Does a Latin-American Transactional Lawyer Do? 36

E. How You Can Pursue a Career in International Law 37

Chapter 5
A Foreign (to the U.S.) Viewpoint on Practicing International Law *41*
by Marcelo Bombau

A. Introduction 41

B. How It All Began 42

C. Suggestions and Tips 43

Part 2
Private Sector *47*

Chapter 6
A Solo Practitioner's Pathway to International Law Practice *49*
by Aaron Schildhaus

A. Introduction 49

B. Entering the Field of International Law 50

C. My Move Abroad 52

D. Returning to the United States and Joining
    the Section of International Law 53

E. My Most Gratifying Professional Experiences 54

F. Conclusion 56

Chapter 7
The Road to an International In-House Legal Career *57*
by Janet Wright and Carolyn Herzog

A. Introduction 57

B. How Did We Get Here and Why Do We Stay? 58

C. Some Thoughts to Consider on Your Path to In-House 60

D. Plan or Chance? 61

E. Thoughts on Finding the Right Fit for You 63

F. Building International Legal and Business Partner Relationships 65

G. Challenges in Networking Outside of Your Company 67

H. Things to Consider in Business Unit Management 68

I. Managing Other Lawyers 70

J. Selecting and Managing Outside Counsel 72

K. Specialization: Benefit or Barrier to Promotion? 74

L. A Few Things You Should Know if You Want to Be General Counsel 76

M. Conclusion 77

Chapter 8

Fair Winds and Following Seas: A Career in Admiralty Practice 79
by Michael Marks Cohen

A. Introduction 79

B. Disadvantages 81

C. Advantages 81

D. Training 83

E. Starting Out 83

Chapter 9

The China Bug 85
by Michael E. Burke

A. Introduction 85

B. Getting Educated 86

C. Law School: What, When, and How? 88

D. Getting a First Job: How, Where, and Why? 90

E. Becoming a Good International Lawyer 91

F. Networking, Associations, and Branding 93

G. Conclusion 94

Chapter 10

A Career in International Commercial Arbitration 95
by Marc J. Goldstein

A. Introduction 95

B. From New York to the Hague   96
C. Choosing a Law Firm   97
D. The Rewards of a Career in International Commercial
    Arbitration   99
    1. *Discovery American-Style*   *100*
    2. *Discovery in International Commercial
        Arbitration*   *100*
    3. *The Quality of Arbitrators*   *101*
    4. *Other Attractions*   *102*
    5. *Over the Long Term*   *103*
E. Advice on Career Preparation   105
F. Where the Road Leads   108

Part 3
Public Sector   *109*

Chapter 11
Practicing International Criminal Law   *111*
by Daryl A. Mundis

A. Introduction   111
B. The Emerging International Criminal Law System   112
C. The Structure of the ICTY and the Functions
    of Its Lawyers   113
    1. *Chambers*   *114*
    2. *Registry*   *114*
    3. *OTP*   *115*
        a. Prosecutions   115
        b. Investigations   115
        c. Legal Advisory Section and Appeals Unit   116
    4. *Defense Counsel*   *116*
D. The Pros and Cons of Life Inside the ICTY   116
E. Some Practical Advice for Law Students   118
    1. *Law School*   *119*
    2. *Graduate School*   *119*
    3. *Study or Living Abroad*   *120*
    4. *Practical Experience*   *121*
    5. *Internships*   *121*

6.	Language Training	122
7.	Networking	123
F.	Conclusion	123

Chapter 12
An International Judge in Kosovo 125
by Hon. Marilyn J. Kaman

A.	Introduction	125
B.	United Nations Mission in Kosovo	127
1.	Some Background	127
2.	Broadening Professional Knowledge and Expertise	128
3.	Professional and Personal Challenges	129
a.	The Cold	129
b.	Intimidation	130
C.	Your Own Career in International Law	131
1.	Career or Calling?	131
2.	Legal Education	132
3.	The Internet	133
4.	Networking	134
5.	Adaptability and Resilience	135
D.	Conclusion	135

Chapter 13
The Practice of International Trade Law in the Public Sector 137
by Eleanor Roberts Lewis

A.	Introduction	137
B.	Why Practice What They Teach?	139
1.	Trade Agreements	139
2.	Trade-Related Legislation, Dispute Settlement, and Litigation	140
3.	Advice and Advocacy for U.S. Exporters and Investors	141
4.	Technical Assistance for Foreign Countries	142
5.	Equal and Better Opportunities	142
C.	Balancing Family and Work	143
1.	Flexible Work Schedules	144
2.	Child Care	144

3. *Medical and Leave Benefits*   145

D. The Disadvantages of Federal Employment   145

E. Opportunities in the Federal Government   146

F. Conclusion   148

Chapter 14
The Journey of a Private Practitioner Who Became an International Rule of Law Attorney   *151*
by Mary Noel Pepys

A. The Journey Begins   151

B. The Substantive Work of International Rule of Law
    Attorneys   153

C. The Diplomatic Work of International Rule of Law
    Attorneys   155

D. Rule of Law Technical Legal Assistant Providers   156

1. *The ABA Rule of Law Initiative*   156

2. *United States Agency for International
    Development (USAID)*   157

3. *The World Bank*   158

4. *The Asia Development Bank, Inter-American
    Development Bank, and the African
    Development Bank*   158

5. *The United Nations Development
    Programme (UNDP)*   158

E. How to Become an International Rule of Law Attorney 159

F. Conclusion   160

Part 4
Practice Tips and Methodology   *161*

Chapter 15
Using the Internet to Develop a Small-Firm International Law Practice   *163*
by Jeffrey M. Aresty and Edward Rholl

A. Introduction   163

B. Working in a Global Legal Environment   164

1. *The Impact of the Internet on the Practice of Law*   164

2. The Complexity of Cyber Law 165
3. New Online Services 165
4. The New Tools of Cyber Lawyers 166

C. How We Use the Internet Effectively
with Foreign Clients 167

D. Our Advice on Career Preparation 169
1. The Tools 170
2. The Skills 170

E. Conclusion 172

Chapter 16
Network or Not Work: The Choice Is Yours 173
by Mark E. Wojcik

A. Introduction 173
B. A Five-Point Checklist 174
1. Look at Your Résumé with the Eyes of an Employer 174
2. Join Professional Associations 177
3. Invite Prospective Employers as Speakers 178
4. Keep Current 179
5. Write Something, and Before You Publish It,
Ask an Expert to Read It 180

C. Getting to Work on Getting Work 181

Chapter 17
Creative Strategies for Launching and Growing
an International Law Practice 183
by Janet H. Moore

A. Introduction 183
B. Responding to Globalization 184
1. Take a Global View 184
2. Become Versatile 184
3. Cultivate Cross-Cultural Competence 185

C. Launching an International Law Career 186
1. Clarify What You Seek 186
2. Conduct a Self-Assessment 186
3. Polish Interview Skills 187
4. Bolster Needed Experience 187

5. *Network Vigorously*   *188*

6 *Research the Culture of Potential Employers*   *189*

7. *Seek International Work Wherever You Land—And Do It Well*   *190*

8. *Ask for What You Want*   *190*

D. Climbing the Career Ladder   190

    1. *Develop Portable Business*   *191*

    2. *Brand Yourself*   *192*

    3. *Connect Daily*   *194*

    4. *Seek Assistance*   *194*

E. Conclusion   195

Chapter 18
One Non-Linear Career in International Law   *197*
by Homer E. Moyer, Jr.

Appendix A
Studying Abroad   *207*

Appendix B
Internet Resources   *221*

Index   *225*

Preface
by Salli A. Swartz

Careers in International Law is now in its third edition and has become a best seller for law students
and lawyers who are interested in a career in international law, irrespective of age, experience, nationality,
residence, or practice area. As you will discover, the
diversity of the careers described in this new edition
is inspiring and exciting and reflects the exponential
increase and depth of opportunities in international
law since the first and second editions of this book
were published.

It is an exciting time to be involved in international law, as it is truly difficult to imagine any cutting-
edge issue in any state or region of the world that is
not affected by some aspect of international law—be it
economic, humanitarian, labor, immigration, commercial, regulatory, insurance, maritime, criminal, trade,
corporate, tax, litigation, alternative dispute resolution, banking, financial, or any of the other new and
emerging areas of international law.

Our authors present many types of creative and
classic career possibilities in both public and private
international law: They are judges and professors;

in-house corporate practitioners; partners with large and small firms and solo practitioners; and employees of government agencies and nongovernmental organizations. These authors are freelance volunteers and consultants, who live and practice law in many different countries and work in many different languages. Despite their different career paths, they have all taken the time to share with you helpful advice and hindsight, which is fascinating reading and indispensable information for anyone contemplating entering or changing careers in the international arena. It has been great fun recruiting the authors and learning about their respective careers, and I hope the testimonials in this edition will inspire our readers to pursue satisfying and enriching careers in international law.

As editor of this new edition, I would like to extend a special thanks to the authors who have shared their insights and advice for their time and patience with my editing. I would also like to extend a special thanks to Rick Paszkiet, deputy director of ABA Book Publishing, without whom this new edition would never have seen the light of day.

with respect to compliance and other issues arising out of the Foreign Corrupt Practices Act, anti-boycott laws, and the OECD Convention on Combating Bribery of Foreign Public Officials. She is regularly lead counsel on due diligence and negotiations in connection with transnational acquisitions and mergers and has over 20 years of experience in international arbitrations (in particular, ICC arbitrations) as well as mediations (she is an accredited mediator with the Chambre de Commerce et Industrie de Paris).

Salli has lectured on "Structuring International Transactions: Establishing Distribution Networks" (Center for International Legal Studies, March 1996); "International Licensing and Competition Law: Know-How Licenses" (Center for International Legal Studies, October 1996); "Doing Business Worldwide: Transnational Litigation" (American Bar Association Midwest International Law Forum, November 1996); "Going International: Distribution and Agency Agreements in Europe" (Virginia Continuing Legal Education Program, May 1997); "Enforcement of Intellectual Property Rights in Madagascar (USIA Guest Speaker, September 1997); "When Disaster Strikes—What to Do When an International Sales Transaction Goes Wrong" (International Bar Association Conference, New Delhi, November 1997); "International Mergers & Acquisitions: Critical Issues for In-House Counsel (American Bar Association Conference, April 1998); "Rights to Privacy Worldwide: Do They Exist, Who Do They Protect and Why" (American Bar Association Conference, April 1998); "Transparency and Business and Government" (Guest Lecturer at the Oman Chamber of Commerce and Industry and the Oman Institute of Public Administration, May 1998); and "Corruption and Transparency in Business and Government" (Guest Lecturer in Burkina Faso, September 1998). She was a Guest Lecturer in both Lomé, Togo and Cotonou, Benin in September 2002 and Addis Ababa, Ethiopia in 2005 on Transparency and Corruption and was a delegate to the ABA International Section International Legal Exchange Program in March 2007 to Accra (Ghana), Monrovia (Liberia), and Freetown (Sierra Leone).

Salli teaches intellectual property at the Ecole National Superieur des Arts & Metiers in Paris and international arbitration and mediation at the French business school Hautes Etudes Commerciales. She has also lectured at several French law and business schools on confidentiality and ethical conflicts between French, European, and American ethical regulations.

She is the author of "Trademark Litigation in France" (Euromoney Publications, September 1996); "Litigation Strategy in France" (Euromoney Publications, March 1997); "Remedies for International Sellers of Goods" (Chapter on France, Sweet & Maxwell, 1997); and "French Language Requirements" (*International Law News*, American Bar Association, Vol. 26 no. 3, Summer 1997). Salli is co-editor and author of a chapter in *Careers in International Law,* published by the ABA in 2001; co-editor of *International Joint Ventures,* published by the ABA in 2002; and author of the chapter "Selling Products in Foreign Countries—International Sales" in the book *Negotiating and Structuring International Commercial Transactions,* published by the ABA in 2003.

She is a member of the Pennsylvania and Paris Bars, with specializations in the Law of International Relations and Commercial Law; is admitted to practice before the French Courts, the U.S. Court of Appeals for the Federal Circuit, the U.S. Court of International Trade, and the U.S. Supreme Court; and is Finance Officer of the International Section of the ABA, of which she is a member of the Governing Council. She is also a member of the Business Law Section of the ABA, an Officer of the Mediation Committee of the International Bar Association, and is the ABA liaison to the Union Internationale des Avocats.

About the Contributors

Jeffrey M. Aresty is a lawyer from Wayland, Massachusetts, and has practiced international business and cyberspace law for 28 years (www.cyberspace attorney.com). During that time, he joined and helped lead a global online network of lawyers in 35 countries, founded a new media company (which distributes interactive web-based training programs for building and sustaining trusted online communities), and led the founding of a virtual bar association (www.internetbar.org). In his volunteer bar work, Jeffrey has run educational programs, published articles and books, and led projects and committees promoting (1) the use of technology in the transformation of the practice of law, and (2) the role of cross-cultural training in international business and e-commerce.

Marcelo Bombau leads the Mergers and Acquisitions, Media and Entertainment, and Customs and Foreign Trade departments of M. & M. Bomchil. Ever since joining M. & M. Bomchil in 1981, he has worked on a number of important transactions, participating actively in some of the most important reorganizations and company purchase deals carried out in Argentina during the last decade, especially related to the media and entertainment areas. Marcelo is a member of the board of directors of several local companies. He has received distinctions in several publications that distinguished him within his area of practice, has written many articles in the area of his expertise, and has lectured both in the Argentine Republic and abroad. Marcelo graduated from Universidad Nacional de La Plata in 1981. He is a member of Colegio de Abogados de la Ciudad de Buenos Aires, the American Bar Association, and the International Bar Association.

Michael E. Burke is a partner with the Washington, D.C. office of Williams Mullen, PC, where he heads the firm's China Practice Group. He earned his BSFS, cum laude, from the Georgetown University School of Foreign Service, where he was selected for the Scholars Program. Mike earned his JD from Georgetown University Law Center. He is an Honorary Fellow with the Asian Institute of International Financial Law. Mike has written more than 40 law review and journal articles and is a frequent speaker on international law issues. He serves as Liaison Officer, Co-Chair of the China Committee, and in other roles for the American Bar Association Section of International Law. Mike is a Fellow of the American Bar Foundation. He is also, proudly, a member of Red Sox Nation.

Michael Marks Cohen has been in private maritime law practice in New York City since 1970, specializing in admiralty law and international arbitration, and is currently of counsel to Nicoletti Hornig & Sweeney. Cohen taught the admiralty course at Columbia Law School for more than 30 years. A Titulary Member of the Comite Maritime International, he is an elected member of the American Law Institute, which honored him with the John Minor Wisdom Award. He is a former member of the Executive Committee of the Maritime Law Association of the United States, a former Development Officer of the ABA International Law Section, and a former member of the Documentary Committee of the Baltic & International Maritime Council (Copenhagen).

Jeffrey Golden is a partner in the London office of international law firm Allen & Overy LLP. He is co-head of Allen & Overy's U.S. law and derivatives practices and has extensive experience in a wide range of capital markets matters, including swaps and derivatives, international equity and debt offerings, U.S. private placements and listings, and mergers, acquisitions and joint ventures. Jeffrey has appeared as an expert witness in several high profile derivatives cases and has served on the American Bar Association's working group on the rule of law and economic development (chair), the Financial Markets Law Committee's working groups on amicus briefs, emergency powers legislation, and *Enron v. TXU* (chair), the Financial Law Panel's working groups on agency dealings by fund managers and other intermediaries and building societies legislation, the Federal Trust's working group on European securities regulation and the European Commission's study group, the City of London joint working group, and ISDA task forces on the legal aspects of monetary union. He is chair of the American Bar Association's Section of International Law, a former co-chair of its International Securities and Capital Markets and U.S. Lawyers Practicing Abroad Committees, and a Fellow of the American Bar Foundation. He also serves on the Commission on the World Justice Project, on the ABA Rule of Law Initiative Board, and as General Editor of the *Capital Markets Law Journal* (Oxford University Press). Jeffrey studied at Duke University, the London School of Economics and Political Science and Columbia University School of Law, from which he received his JD degree with honors in 1978.

Marc J. Goldstein established his own law firm in March 2007 after a 26-year career in large law firms in New York. He is currently vice-chair of the Canada Committee of the ABA Section of International Law and Practice, and was formerly co-chair of its dispute resolution and litigation committees. He devotes most of his time to international arbitration (as an arbitrator and advocate) and international litigation, and frequently writes and speaks on those topics.

Carolyn Herzog is Senior Director in Symantec Corporation's global legal department. In her current role, Herzog provides the primary legal support for Symantec's Global Services and Support (GSS) organization to enable the development and implementation of GSS initiatives, including establishment of strategic alliances, creation and publication of corporate policies and compliance programs, acquisition and development of assets and technology transfers through M&A, joint ventures, joint research and development arrangements, and revenue creation through distribution, licensing, manufacturing, supply, and service arrangements. Herzog also supervises the legal support for trade compliance policies and practice. Prior to joining Symantec, Herzog was the Acting General Counsel for AXENT Technologies, Inc. in Rockville, MD, and Staff Attorney for the International Law Institute in Washington, D.C.

Bruce Horowitz was born and raised in the town of Galion, Ohio, and went to college and law school in the United States. After living in Ecuador for 25 years, Horowitz considers both Ecuador and the United States as home. He is a founder and managing partner of the PAZ HOROWITZ, Abogados law firm in Quito. Bruce is a long-time member of the American Bar Association, and has been active in the ABA International Section and its International IP, Latin American & Caribbean, Lawyers Abroad, and Anti-Corruption Committees. He is also active in the International Trademark Association (INTA) and local conservation organizations. He continues to enjoy international IP work, and is concentrating particularly on advising and training clients and client groups on strategies and techniques to deter extortion by government functionaries.

Judge Marilyn J. Kaman, a state court trial judge for the 4th Judicial District in Hennepin County, Minnesota since 1990, was selected in 2002 by the United Nations to become an International Judge for the United Nations Mission in Kosovo and one of the first four American jurists to serve for the United Nations abroad. Judge Kaman has extensive experience as a trial court judge, with emphasis on major criminal trials and major civil litigation. Additionally, she has served in specialty court judicial assignments for probate, mental health, and family court divisions of the Court. Judge Kaman is a member of the American Bar Association, Section of International Law, and holds the following appointments: Co-Chair, International Criminal Law Committee; Deputy Editor, *International Law News;* Co-Chair, U. N. &

International Institutions Coordinating Committee; Co-Chair, ILEX-Liberia Africa Task Force. Judge Kaman is one of the American Bar Association's Representatives to the United Nations Economic & Social Council.

Eleanor Roberts Lewis was Chief Counsel for International Commerce at the U.S. Department of Commerce from 1982 until 2006. She was personally involved in the negotiation, implementation and enforcement of many international trade and investment agreements. Eleanor also worked on other important initiatives including the modernization of commercial law in developing countries. Before coming to the Department of Commerce, Eleanor worked at the U.S. Department of Housing & Urban Development and spent three years in private law practice in Washington, D.C. She has a BA from Wellesley College, an MA from Harvard University, and a J.D. from Georgetown University.

Andrew J. Markus is a shareholder at Carlton Fields, P.A., located in its Miami office. He is the chair of the International Practice Group of the firm. He is also a Past Chair of the ABA's Section of International Law and one of two delegates named by the Section to the House of Delegates of the ABA. His practice involves representing U.S. and non-U.S. companies in the U.S. and worldwide in international and domestic corporate transactions, including joint ventures, strategic alliances, mergers and acquisitions, and financial transactions. Andrew frequently coordinates multijurisdictional projects for major U.S. and non-U.S. companies.

Janet H. Moore, JD, ACC, practiced law (international business transactions) for 15 years before becoming a trainer, consultant, and professionally trained and certified executive coach for lawyers. Through her company, International Lawyer Coach, Inc. (www.InternationalLawyerCoach.com), Janet helps lawyers thrive in our global economy with customized rainmaking, branding, and career strategies.

Homer E. Moyer, Jr. is a partner at Miller & Chevalier, where he founded the firm's International Department and manages a diverse international regulatory and litigation practice. A former Chair of the Section of International Law, Homer was the co-founder and Chair of CEELI, the ABA's Central European and Eurasian Law Initiative, and the founder of the CEELI Institute in Prague. A political appointee in both Democratic and Republican administrations, Homer served as General Counsel, Counselor to the Secretary, and Deputy General Counsel of the U.S. Department of Commerce. Before government, he practiced with Covington & Burling; wrote *Justice and the Military,* a treatise on military law; and served in Navy JAG, with collateral duty at the White House. He has received the ABA's World Order Under Law Award and was honored at Runnymede during the rededication of the ABA Memorial to Magna Carta. A member of the Council on Foreign Relations, past President of the Washington Council of Lawyers, and father of four, he also authored the best-selling book, *The R.A.T. (Real-World Aptitude Test): Preparing Yourself for Leaving Home* (Capital Books; 2001).

Daryl A. Mundis is a senior prosecuting trial attorney with the Office of the Prosecutor ("OTP") at the International Criminal Tribunal for the former Yugoslavia. He has been on the prosecution team in a number of cases and prior to joining the OTP, he worked in the Chambers of Judge Gabrielle Kirk McDonald, the second ICTY President. Daryl also served for more than five years in the U.S. Navy JAG Corps, including stints as both prosecutor and defense counsel. He may be contacted at mundis.icty@un.org.

Mary Noel Pepys is a senior attorney with a specialization in the rule of law, specifically international legal and judicial reform, and most recently corruption within the judiciary. Mary has years of legal experience in the judicial, legislative, diplomatic, and private sectors, and has lived and worked abroad within former communist countries, the Middle East, Asia, and Western Europe. With her knowledge of common law and civil law principles, she has successfully developed, managed, and implemented effective legal reform projects, promoting transparent and fair justice systems in more than 30 countries. She has worked with USAID, The World Bank, U.S. and foreign embassies, numerous international organizations, and diverse foreign NGOs to provide legal and technical assistance to national governments, judiciary, bar, and law faculties.

Edward Rholl is currently acting as executive director of Internet Bar and is a member of the faculty of the Internet Bar Institute. He is also founder and president of Transformative Law, a certified continuing legal education provider in the state of California. Edward is a graduate of Marquette University Law School (JD) and Georgetown University Law School (LL.M), was a practicing lawyer from 1992–1998, and has spent the past several years researching, writing, and training lawyers in the fields of business development, marketing, and technology issues. He lives and works in San Diego, California.

Aaron Schildhaus is an international corporate and business lawyer specializing in commercial transactions, trade, and finance. He has written and lectured on international relations, policy, and trade throughout the U.S., Europe, Africa, the Middle East, and Asia. Schildhaus has extensive corporate and legal experience representing major multinational corporations, as well as small and medium-sized investors, based in Europe, the United States, and elsewhere, with respect to transnational corporate strategy, international sales and distribution, transborder business alliances and joint ventures, and international transactions and trade in the United States and abroad. Aaron was a member of the corporate law department of PepsiCo, Inc. for three years before moving to Paris in 1975, where he practiced for the next 10 years. He was founder and president of The International Business Law Firm and The European Business Law Firm, and was of counsel to the firm of Carlsmith Ball in its Washington, D.C. office. Since 1996, he has been in private practice in Washington, D.C.

Mark E. Wojcik is a professor of law and Director of Global Legal Studies at The John Marshall Law School in Chicago, where he has taught Public International Law, International Business Transactions, International Trade Law, International Human Rights, and Lawyering Skills. He also teaches at the University of Lucerne

Faculty of Law in Lucerne, Switzerland and at the Facultad Libre de Derecho de Monterrey in Mexico. Mark is also the Director of Legal English at the International Law Institute in Washington, D.C. He serves as Publications Officer for the ABA Section of International Law and as Editor-in-Chief of the section's newsletter, *The International Law News.* He has also been a chair of the Association of American Law Schools Section on North American Cooperation, Section on International Human Rights Law, Section on Graduate Programs for Foreign Lawyers, and Section on International Legal Exchange. Mark previously chaired the Illinois State Bar Association Section on International and Immigration Law and now serves on the ISBA Board of Governors. He is also chair of the American Society of International Law Interest Group in Teaching International Law.

Janet B. Wright is Director of HSB | DIS Legal. Her responsibilities include legal support for Dell's U.S. consumer and small business sales segments and the related global customer contact centers, as well as global privacy matters. In her prior role at Dell, she was Director for Corporate Legal, responsible for general corporate and securities matters, domestic and international tax matters, domestic and international equity compensation, employee benefits programs, and other corporate legal work. Prior to joining Dell, Janet spent 10 years in private practice. During that period, she focused on mergers and acquisitions, equity structuring and choice of entity issues, international and domestic tax work, and tax controversy work. She is a member of the ABA Section of International Law and Practice and the Tax Section. She is the former chair of the International Section's Women's Interest Network.

Profile of the ABA Section of International Law

Who Are We?

- We are over **19,500 members:**
- **More than 50% of our members are in private practice:** The top three areas of practice: business law, litigation, and intellectual property.
  - Corporate Counsel – more than 12% are U.S. members
  - Government Lawyers – 3% are U.S. members
  - Academics – 4% are U.S. members
- **You don't have to be a U.S. lawyer to be a member of the Section!**

Where Are We?

- **U.S. lawyers in the U.S. (top 5):** Washington, D.C., New York, California, Texas, and Illinois
- **U.S. lawyers abroad (top 5):** United Kingdom, Japan, France, Canada, and Germany

- **Non-U.S. lawyer abroad (top 5):** Canada, United Kingdom, Mexico, Germany, and Australia

What Do We Do?

We serve our members, the profession and the public through:

- **Continuing Legal Education:** Seasonal meetings; standalone; committee programs (e.g., the annual "Live from the SEC" videoconference; trade law conferences such as "The World Trade Organization at 10 and the Road to Hong Kong" and the Jackson International Trade Seminar, National Institute on Economic Sanctions and Export Controls Conferences, and public international law conferences, most recently on "The Nuremberg Trials and the Birth of International Law")

- **Member Publications:** *The International Lawyer*, the most widely-circulated law review/law journal on international law in the world; the *International Law News,* a quarterly magazine; and 24 committee newsletters relating to International Human Rights, Latin American/Caribbean, China, Asia/Pacific, International Family Law, and International Commercial Transactions

- **Book Publications** on international practice issues

- Over **60 substantive committees in 12 divisions,** with active listserves facilitating current information exchange among experts in the specific areas covered by the committees

- **ABA United Nations Development Program International Legal Resource Center**

- **International Outreach to the Global Legal Community:**
  - We organize ABA Day at the United Nations
  - We have liaisons to the World Trade Organization, as well as to Foreign and International Bars
  - We send delegations on International Legal Exchange (ILEX) trips, and have visited 45 countries since 1982
  - Annual International Bar Leaders Trips: Our Section Leaders travel to different countries to meet with and develop relationships and cooperate with foreign

bars. To date, we have visited bars in Asia, Europe, and South America.

- We send delegations to significant World Conferences, e.g., WTO Conference, Sustainable Development (Johannesburg, 2002); International Criminal Court (Rome, 1998); International Conference on Women (Beijing, 1998)

- **Interaction with the U.S. Government:**
  - Annual dinner of General Counsels of U.S. Government Departments and Agencies
  - Section "Day on the Hill" every other year
  - State Department Lawyers on Section Council
  - Advice on nominations to international courts

- **Policy Developer and Advocate**
  - Numerous reports and recommendations that create official ABA policy (e.g., the Universal Jurisdiction, Terrorism, Foreign Intelligence Surveillance Act; Money Laundering/Gatekeeper Regulations; and the Foreign Sovereign Immunities Act)
  - Blanket Authority Comments

Part

Foreign Practice

1

Demystifying the Career of an International Derivatives Lawyer

by Jeffrey B. Golden[1]

1

A. Introduction

What an exciting time to be contemplating a career in international law! In private practice, it was not always like this. Thirty years ago, interviewing for an associate's position with the leading Wall Street firms, I had to apologize for my interest in international law. Senior partners at the firms that I visited denied the relevance of international law and practice. However, all that has changed. International is where it is at. These days, the law firms on Wall Street, like

---

[1] Chair of the American Bar Association Section of International Law. Partner and Co-head of the U.S. Law Group and Derivatives Practice Group, Allen & Overy LLP.

elsewhere, are determined to convince recruits that their practices on offer are truly international.

The choices and opportunities certainly seemed more limited when I graduated from law school. I joined New York law firm Cravath, Swaine & Moore, which at least showed two overseas branch offices on its letterhead. When, after five years in the New York office, I was offered a posting to London, I grabbed it. My wife is English, and we were thrilled. Not everyone thought this was a career-enhancing move, however. Another associate queried the logic of my transferring to what he described as an outpost. I replied that the senior partner had assured me that the plan was to expand the London office, but my colleague was unconvinced. "What are they going to do?" he asked. "Add another Rapifax machine?"

In fact, with my arrival in London, the size of the Cravath office there was increased by 50 percent—from two to three lawyers. In an office that size, it was probably inevitable that I would be stretched by a broad range of transactional experience, including, in this case, capital markets, banking, general corporate, joint venture, and, especially, merger and acquisition work. Looking back, that stretching was not an altogether bad thing.

In the early 1980s, our client, Salomon Brothers, came to us seeking documentation and legal advice in connection with a new financial product—a swap—which derived its value from movements in prices in underlying interest rate and currency markets. There was not much competition among our colleagues for this novel work, out of the Cravath mainstream as it was ("If it is important, we would already be doing it"), but Dan Cunningham, a partner in the Cravath New York office (and now my partner at Allen & Overy LLP), and I were fascinated by the opportunity and the dynamic investment bankers we were mixing with in this fledgling market. Maybe it was the Concorde flights. Because very few lawyers understood the business, those of us who did were being flown back and forth between New York and London on very fast airplanes. Deadlines were tight, but the substantial margins for these deals in the early days of the business allowed for some serious celebrations when the deadlines were met and the deals closed.

However, different lawyers in different rooms and at different times had produced different forms of swap agreements for their respective banks, and the conflicts these gave rise to and the costs of the lengthy negotiations that followed were a real impediment to the growth of the business. To avoid a "battle of the forms," Dan and I were asked by Salomon Brothers and other leading market participants to attempt to harmonize the various agreement precedents then being used. The code of contract terms that we produced and the master agreement that followed from it became the industry's standard. We have continued to advise the International Swaps and Derivatives Association (ISDA) since in the development of the ISDA Master Agreement, which I am told now supports more than $400 trillion notional amount trading today. So I hope that we got the contract right!

The law students whom I interview sometimes ask me, "How was it, when you were a 2L, that you knew you wanted to pursue a career in derivatives or the law of corporate finance?" Well, as you can see, I did not and, in the case of derivatives, could not know since the underlying business had not been invented. In fact, I did not have much of an idea what lay ahead or what were the distinguishing features of the practices of lawyers in big law firms. When I turned up for my first day at Cravath, a stern lady came out of the personnel office and confronted me with the question, "Which department, corporate or litigation?" "Which one is the IBM case?" I asked. "That's litigation," she replied. "Right," I said. "I'll take corporate." And my whole career followed from that.

In any event, after more than 15 years at Cravath and 10 years into what was meant to be an 18-month stint in the Cravath London office, I had come to know well, through my M&A and derivatives work, the leading so-called Magic Circle English law practices. When the rules that had prevented English law qualified solicitors from partnering with non-English law qualified lawyers were relaxed, one of these firms, Allen & Overy, got brave and decided to put together an English and U.S. law capability under one roof. A&O approached me and asked if I would come across the street, join them as their first non-English law qualified partner, and start up the firm's U.S. law practice. The lure of taking that road less well traveled by was irresistible. That was 1994. And the rest, as they say, is history.

The Allen & Overy U.S. Law Group that I remember consisting of one lawyer sitting in London—the only non-English law qualified partner—is now a diversified global U.S. law practice of more than 250 U.S. law qualified lawyers in a firm with more lawyers outside the United Kingdom than in it and more non-English law qualified partners than English law qualified ones. More than 2,500 lawyers overall are practicing out of 28 cities literally around the globe. My partners include (in addition to British and Americans) French, German, Dutch, Spanish, Italian, Polish, Russian, Chinese, and Japanese lawyers. A lot has changed in the last decade. Why wasn't this on offer when I came out of law school?

So, exciting times. Many of you reading this book will be too young to have been, like me, a university student in the revolutionary 1960s. You missed that. Too bad. It was great. However, this may be about as exciting, and revolutionary, a time as the legal profession has known—especially if you are interested in a career in international law! But now let me share a few secrets about derivatives and how to pursue a career as a derivatives lawyer.

B.   Why Derivatives Are Relevant

I remember being a terrible embarrassment to my daughter at a school event a couple of years ago. She had a leading role in the student production of *Joseph and the Amazing Technicolor Dreamcoat*. My wife and I sat proudly in the front row. There is that bit in the plot when the Pharaoh is asking Joseph to explain the Pharaoh's dreams, and there is dialogue along the lines of "Seven fat cows, seven thin cows—Joseph, what does it mean? . . . Seven good years, seven bad years—Joseph, what can I do?" I shouted out from the front row: "Derivatives!" I can still remember my daughter, hands on hip, glaring back at me.

Well, like the good bard said, "All the world's a stage," and a few months later it was as if the theatre lights were back on and I had been projected right into the plot of *Joseph*. In the Middle East, as part of a small delegation from the American Bar Association Section of International Law, I found myself in meetings in Damascus with Syria's Minister of Planning. He was lamenting the fact that Syria had just experienced a long period of drought, which could easily lead to famine. "Drought, famine, and I'm the Minister for Planning," he said. "But how can you plan for such things? How can you be expected to deal at the time with the extraordinary costs? What am I to do?"

This time I didn't shout. But slowly, my hand went up. "Have you heard of weather derivatives?" I asked when the Minister looked my way. "Put somewhat crudely," I explained, "your nightmare is the dream of some ice cream vendor or some air-conditioner manufacturer who can look to, but could not have counted on, record sales in what turns out to be a long, hot, and dry season. Still, next year's weather might be very different. Derivatives are a means of bringing your competing interests together, because each of you may be prepared to swap some of your upside in what would be a good year for the protection of a payout to help you cope with the risks of an unusually bad year."

C. What Are Derivatives?

A derivative is a contract that derives its value from something else. For example, like the weather derivative example, the value of the contract might rise or fall depending on whether the temperature rises or falls or based on how many sunny days there are in a relevant period. Similarly, an option on a share of IBM or BT is a contract that derives its value from, among other things, the price of an IBM or BT share, as the case may be. Derivatives can be private, bilateral contracts (called *over-the-counter* or OTC transactions) or take the form of securities that are publicly traded on an exchange (i.e., listed options and futures).

D.   Why Do You Do It?

Parties enter into derivatives contracts for a variety of reasons, but generally they are designed to manage or tailor a party's risk exposure. For example:

- If you want to decrease your exposure (risk) to interest rate movements in relation to a loan portfolio that pays interest at a floating rate, you can enter into a swap with another party, where you make payments to the counterparty based on the floating-rate interest payments you receive on the loans, and the counterparty makes payments to you based on a fixed rate. In essence, this turns your floating-rate assets into fixed-rate assets and consequently reduces your risk to interest rate movements.
- If you want to increase your exposure or risk in respect of the S&P 500 or the Footsie 100 (because you think the index is going to rise), you can enter into options or swaps that make payments based on the level of the index.

E.   What Does It Involve?

Derivatives as a practice area sounds like it is a specialized or niche practice, but in many respects it is the last great generalist practice. A good derivatives lawyer will need to develop skills to deal with the following:

- Legal issues relating to contracts, secured credit, securities and commodities regulation, insolvency, conflicts of law, tax, banking, dispute resolution, and the list goes on
- Structuring issues like matching cash flows and allocating risks between the parties
- Disaster management (ever heard of Nick Leeson? Also see Asia in 1997 and Russia in 1998)
- Business development issues like helping clients to establish new Web-based trading platforms

- Legislating and regulating for systemic risk, given the global nature of the business and its scale

F. When Does It Get Interesting?

Given the variety of the work, the sums involved (at last count, the OTC derivatives market alone measured US$400 trillion in notional amount trading), and the fast pace of the industry, it's always interesting. When something big happens, like the Russian crisis in 1998, you get to be at the heart of some real headline-grabbing stuff.

G. One Last Tip

As part of the training for new members in our firm's Derivatives Group, we have historically run an introductory lecture entitled "How to Succeed at a Derivatives Cocktail Party without Really Trying." The reason given for this program is that, in light of the depth and three-dimensional nature of our derivatives practice, even young lawyers can expect to fairly quickly find themselves meeting (in some cases, socially) with clients and other leaders in this field. It is important for the junior lawyer (and for the firm) that he or she is a good advertisement for our practice. Accordingly, in this first lecture, each new lawyer is given a small piece of paper, of a size that would fit into the palm of your hand, with five one-liners on it that can be dropped casually into conversations at a cocktail party. Each one-liner is designed to impress, and four of them vary from year to year. These reflect topical themes, so that this year there might be one on credit derivatives or on collateral reform and efforts to harmonize the various jurisdictional laws on the taking of security, or on "flawed asset theory" and the recent Australian court decision in the Enron case.

But the fifth one-liner never varies from year to year, and it is always just one word long: "Netting." We tell our young lawyers that if all else is forgotten, they should just remember: "Netting."

Whatever the question, they can always answer, "Netting." (Why master agreements? Netting. Why special-purpose vehicles? Netting.) It will either be the right answer or, in any event, the person putting the question, knowing netting to be both so important and so complicated, will be too intimidated to second-guess the answer.[2] So, if you are in that all-important interview, seeking to be a derivatives lawyer, and you are at a loss for something that will impress . . . just remember "Netting"!

---

[2] "Netting" (and more particularly, "close-out netting") refers to a contractually agreed, and in some cases statutorily supported, basis for calculating or liquidating a single claim for settling or valuing the parties' broader derivatives trading relationship. The parties may have entered into any number of derivatives trades over time, and, at any particular time, some of these trades may be "in-the-money" for one of the parties while, for it, other trades may be "out-of-the-money." Where the parties intend that their credit relationship should be viewed as "net," they will likely trade derivatives subject to the terms of standard form agreements that contemplate close-out netting when the trading relationship terminates. When that happens, the value of all outstanding trades is calculated, the pluses of the in-the-money trades are offset against the minuses of the out-of-the-money trades, and only the difference can be claimed. When one of the parties is bankrupt, netting prevents a liquidator from cherry-picking and making payments on transactions that are favorable and profitable for the insolvent party and refusing to make payments for transactions that are not profitable.

Netting is relevant for two closely related but somewhat different reasons: (1) *as an assessment of credit risk* (the enforceability of netting will determine the measure of exposure to a counterparty and the measure of the claim that can be asserted in subsequent court proceedings if the counterparty is insolvent), and (2) *as an assessment of capital costs* for regulated financial institutions (the amount of capital that a bank must set aside as the cost of engaging in its derivatives business will turn on whether the bank's regulator recognizes the enforceability of its netting arrangements). It has been estimated that netting can reduce a party's exposure to its counterparty by anywhere from 40 to 60 percent. With the notional amount of OTC derivatives trading in the system currently estimated to be in the order of US$400 trillion, that is potentially a lot of credit and systemic risk reduction!

How Do You Get from Philadelphia to Paris?

2

by Salli A. Swartz

A. Introduction

Other than the fact that both cities start with the same letter and I was born in one and live in the other, the practice of law in Philadelphia and Paris is as different as a Philly steak sandwich and a steak frites. They both have meat and a baguette-like bread, but they do not taste anything alike. After living and working in Paris for the last 28 years, I still ask myself how I got here and how I did what I did.

For those readers who have not read the second edition of this book, I will summarize my unpredictable and unforseeable career path and then reflect on the bigger picture, which hopefully will give you some insight into your current and future career paths.

B. The Beginnings

I was always fascinated with Europe and international law and had spent my junior year abroad in

Paris. I fully intended to find a way to live and work abroad; I just didn't know if it was law that would provide the ticket to get there. Although I was seriously interested in international law as a career option, I dropped it in about 10 minutes when I considered my options upon graduation from law school in 1977.

At that time and at my law school, there were only a few courses in international law, and they concentrated on public international law. The law school did offer a certificate in International Legal Studies for those who took all of the courses, which I obtained. I was also the Lead Articles Editor of the *Journal of International Law and Commerce*. However, the only job recruiters who came to the school were the New York corporate firms, which were not interested in anyone who wanted to practice international law, unless it was after seven years of learning the ropes in mergers and acquisitions (M&A), corporate taxation, and litigation. Public international law jobs were almost nonexistent, and working for the government at the height of the Vietnam era was not on my agenda.

So I put the idea of a career in international law aside, thinking that I would make it into a hobby by reading and doing pro bono work. Instead, I became a legal services attorney in rural Pennsylvania. But it is funny how things turn out. The ticket to Europe wasn't law, it was love: I married a French engineer and agreed to go with him to Paris while he was being trained by the French parent company of his U.S. employer.

End of fantasy, beginning of struggle.

C. The Struggle

How do you obtain employment in a country where your language skills can just about get you through the market and the appetizer at a dinner party, but not through a serious job interview, never mind any legal research or writing? How do you obtain a job with a corporate law firm when your only background is U.S. poverty law? How do you get admitted to practice when there are two professions, *conseil juridique* and *avocat*, and the former required gainful employment with an existing firm of *conseil juridique* and at least three years' prior practice and the latter required French nationality and a French bar exam? How do you do all of this with no mentors and no contacts? The only answer I came up with at the time was to send out 200 résumés, call everyone in the phone book, and be persistent. I even knocked on doors. (Note: This is not a good idea.) This was before the Internet and even before computers. The choices were slim.

D. The Breakthrough

After two weeks, I had my first offer: babysitting the telephones, faxes, and telex for a firm of two lawyers, both of whom were going on vacation—it was August in Paris—and I took it. After one month, I had an offer to do expatriate tax returns with Peat Marwick. I took it. After eight weeks, I resigned from the tax position and accepted an offer as an international arbitration paralegal with an Anglo-Saxon law firm in Paris. Not great for an attorney with three years of experience, but my foot was in the door, and at the time, anything looked better to me than sitting on the 22nd floor of a skyscraper in the La Defense part of Paris filling out tax forms for expatriates.

After three months at the law firm and several persuasive arguments, I was promoted from paralegal to attorney. After six months, I was interviewing witnesses in Finland and drafting claims for an International Chamber of Commerce (ICC) construction arbitration in the Middle East. After two years, I was formally admitted to practice as a foreign *conseil juridique* and had the official working papers to go with the title. After four years, I was knee-deep in technical construction claims in several ICC construction arbitrations in the Middle East and realized that I needed to learn French corporate and commercial law. I decided to resign and look for a position with a French firm of *avocats*.

In those four long years, I had progressed from a paralegal position to an experienced ICC arbitration attorney and now had sufficient confidence, language skills, and cultural and legal knowledge to obtain a position with a French firm of *avocats*. I no longer felt like an American duck out of water. I had become

Parisian. Eureka! I screamed with joy. I had finally made it—or so I thought.

E. Success Is Just Around the Corner

Changing firms, not unlike changing spouses (not that I have any experience), is always interesting, particularly when you do it on the rebound. The firm I joined was a small boutique firm with three partners. I was only the second American, and the first one was writing a Matthew Bender publication *Doing Business in France* for the firm. When the book was finished, he left the firm.

I understood that I was hired to be an associate who would work on client files with other attorneys and the clients they represented; they understood that I would be the linguistic specialist and would spend my days correcting English-language documents drafted by the French (male) attorneys, who did not take kindly to corrections. So much for clear communications.

The firm was chauvinistic and somewhat anti-American: This was France in the 1980s. I was told by one partner one evening when I was working late to go home and cook dinner for my husband; another partner informed me that he could not put me on the arbitration team because the client did not want to work with a woman. Ah, the joys of working in a foreign environment. Despite the setbacks and frustrations, in the next four years I spent with that firm, I learned the inside of French corporate, labor, and commercial law, and my written and spoken French became fluent, albeit accented. It was an essential step, even if it wasn't exactly the perfect fit.

I left that firm for several reasons to join an offshoot of Price Waterhouse, where I was a senior attorney. The experience was interesting and challenging, but there I was with an accounting firm again. Not my cup of tea. What was my next step?

F. The Jump to Independence

When a friend and colleague was admitted as an *avocat*, she suggested that we start a firm. I burst out laughing at the mere suggestion that I could earn a living on my own. Six months later, we were profitable, and although the firm has grown and moved and my original partner is long gone, it is still independent and successful almost 20 years later.

One of the reasons I believe my firm has been so successful and has lasted so long is that my focus and expectations were always very clear. Having experienced several different types of legal practices, I knew what I wanted: independence and an exciting and varied practice. I was much less interested in firm politics, money, security, and power than with the challenge of every day being a new learning experience. Flexibility, adaptability, and loyalty to my clients were and are the keys to my success. I have always focused on what I think is the most important part of a law practice: making the client happy by being efficient, amiable, and business-like. Solve the client's problem efficiently, intelligently, and with good humor, and you cannot go wrong.

In line with my objectives, my practice has varied over the years with the one underlying constant: diversity. I have not specialized and do not intend to do so. I go where my clients want to go, and I specialize in their activities.

The matters I have handled have varied over the years and include:

- Purchasing and leasing of aircraft for a new Middle East airline
- Finding and negotiating the purchase of chateaux and other high-end real estate for foreign individuals, including a vineyard in Burgundy
- Consortia agreements for the construction of military airbases
- Hydrocarbon exploration and exploitation agreements for oil and natural gas fields in Africa and the Middle East
- Complex international software framework license agreements
- Capital risk investments and licensing arrangements for high-tech start-ups

- Construction contacts for high-speed motor boats for a government and a luxury sailboat for an individual
- Distribution, joint venture, and agency agreements
- Conducting international arbitrations as counsel and as arbitrator
- Acting as a mediator
- Litigating labor lawsuits and intellectual property infringement cases
- Negotiating with French unions in lockout and strike situations
- Mergers and acquisitions of French companies by Anglo-Saxon companies
- Acquisitions by French companies of Swiss, African, German, Austrian, Italian, English, American, Israeli, Indian, and other foreign companies
- Teaching international arbitration and mediation and intellectual property in French business and engineering schools

I have met interesting people in interesting places. I have traveled to the Middle East covered from head to toe in black. I have eaten alone in restaurants and was mistaken for a woman of the night in the coffee shop at the Hilton in Rotterdam, The Netherlands, in 1981. I have listened to jokes about women, Jews, racial minorities, and other off-color and not-very-funny remarks. I have tried to get a sense of conversations in languages I did not understand by watching the eyebrows, hands, and feet of the speakers. I hitchhiked a ride to the airport when my clients forgot me at the hotel and the taxis were on strike. I have been sequestered by unions that occupied a factory. I have eaten unrecognizable items and slept in less-than-ideal hotels.

But I have never (well, almost never) been bored and delight in the fact that I am constantly learning about new laws, new issues, new languages, and new cultures. It's a challenge and can be exhausting, but most days, I would not trade it for any other profession in any other country.

G. How to Prepare for a Career in International Law

As you prepare for a career in international law, you will need to consider what type of international law you want to practice, in what environment, and what type of lifestyle.

1. What Is International Law?

You can't prepare for something if you don't know what it is. I will share a secret with you: A career in international law means something different to every one of us who are in the field. It could mean working in a law firm in a foreign country, or working in a law firm in the United States and dealing with foreign clients, or negotiating deals between clients located in two different countries as either in-house counsel for a multinational company or as an attorney with a law firm with clients based in different countries in the world.

It can also mean working for a U.S. government agency dealing in international public law matters, such as the State Department, or international private law matters, such as the Commerce Department, or it could mean working in the military as a Judge Advocate General (JAG) officer, or for a nongovernmental organization (NGO) abroad, or as a staff attorney with a United Nations organization, such as ILO, WHO, WIPO, or UNESCO. It can also mean being part of the defense or prosecutorial team(s) of the International Criminal Court, or a staff attorney with the International Chamber of Commerce, or a professor of law who teaches and writes scholarly articles on cutting-edge issues of the law. One thing is certain: there are as many options out there as there are creative ways of practicing law.

The trick is to examine what interests you in the words *international* and *law*. Is it travel? Is it languages? Is it the complexity of dealing with different legal systems and cultures? Is it human rights? Is it being in an environment where you may be intellectually challenged until you retire or die? Only you know the answer. Once you know what interests you, then you need to find an environment that is conducive to doing what you want to do.

2.   In What Type of Environment Do I Want to Practice?

The environment in which you practice can be as important as the type of law you practice. Ask yourself the following questions:

- Do you do well in large bureaucracies, or do you feel that you will scream if someone requires another form to fill out in order to obtain a new hard drive for your computer?
- Do you like small and intimate working environments where you might have to do some photocopying and call your own taxi from time to time, or do you feel claustrophobic and inopportuned just thinking about it?
- Do you want lots of human contact and consider yourself a people person, or would you rather communicate with books and computers?
- Do you like to have an audience (such as in litigation or lecturing), or would you rather hide in a closet?
- Do you like cocktail parties and public relations events, or would you rather spend your evenings in the library?
- Do you like not knowing what each day will bring, or does the uncertainty bring on an anxiety attack?
- Do you like to travel and are always prepared to leave town, or do you get depressed every time you see a suitcase?

The list can go on and on, but I am sure you get the point. It is not just the intellectual gray matter that counts, but the environment in which you will use your gray matter that is as, or more, important.

3.   What Are My Lifestyle Choices?

Not all careers will give you choices with regard to where you live and the hours you work. In-house positions can be as time consuming and stressful as law firm positions. Do not make any assumptions when interviewing and making choices about which position to accept. Being independent can help or hinder, depending on how you organize your life and what type of practice you have.

If you have made certain decisions about lifestyle choices, then you should be very clear about them. For example, I always wanted to have a full-time legal career and had no guilt attacks when juggling work and family, although I did have a lot of headaches and didn't get a manicure very often! Women and men who want to have a full-time career and a family life should be prepared to obtain good and reliable organizational support to manage the stress level for late nights, weekends, and unexpected and prolonged travel.

I had it somewhat easy because French labor laws are very friendly to women who want to work and still have a family. European employers generally tend to be supportive of mothers who work, although your career may take longer to develop if you have a baby a year. In France, paid maternity leave is obligatory for women employees, and it is currently 10 weeks for the first child and increases thereafter per additional child. Moreover, you can add the annual five weeks' French vacation to the maternity leave, so that women can be absent and paid for 15 weeks in the year you give birth. Men can also take parental leaves of absence, although they are less remunerated than maternity leave. Child care is subsidized by the state, and most large urban areas have maternal assistants, nursury schools, and other collective child care facilities so that you can find child care adapted to your lifestyle and budget.

It also helps to have a supportive—and I mean that in all senses of the word—spouse who is prepared to assume and oversee the household tasks, including the really exciting tasks like dry cleaning, food shopping, and paying the bills, when the other spouse is traveling, working all night, or just generally exhausted. It also helped having a spouse who had a full-time, dependable position when I started my own firm, as well as a good sense of humor and an ability to see options when I saw none. My husband and I often realized we would both be out of town on business trips with a three-year-old at home and no food in the house. The trick is getting your priorities right and focusing on what is the most important issue during any given crisis—and not losing sight of the fact that this is the life you have chosen.

My advice is that it is all feasible, but you need to be very organized and willing to compromise on how your time is spent and with whom. Most important, you need to be able to be happy with your choices so that you do not spend your days and nights second-guessing yourself and feeling guilty.

H. Lessons Learned

We all have hindsight after the fact and are very good at ignoring and forgetting it. Here are a few lessons that I carry with me to this day.

1. Compromises in Job Choices

If you are going to make them—and please, get over it, everyone makes them—try to be very clear-sighted about what compromises you are making and why you are making them before you make them. (See the previous discussion on lifestyle choices.) If you are not honest with yourself and do not take the time to adequately reflect on and get insight into your motivations, intentions, and expectations, as well as your strengths and weaknesses, you will find yourself frustrated and disappointed. This may take some work on your part, but it is well worth the time and effort, and it should be a continual process to be carried out before, during, and after each choice and change.

2. Manage Expectations

Go easy on yourself. Keep your expectations in line with reality. If you expect too much, you will indeed be disappointed, probably frustrated, and possibly angry. Do not oversell yourself to either yourself or others. It is better for your employer/partner/associates to be happily surprised than unhappily disappointed. Do not let anyone know that you think you are more intelligent than your boss, even if, in fact, you are. Presumptuousness is not a good idea if you are under the age of 50, and even then . . . .

Take the time to take stock of the situation you are in and the one you would like to be in. Are you fulfilled? Satisfied? Are your feelings and expectations and dreams based on reality? Feasible? What do you need to be doing to get where you want to be going? Be truthful and frank and discuss your insights and ideas with those of your close circle of friends and family who know you the best. And find and use a mentor.

3. Find Mentors and Join Associations

Do not try to go it alone. I did not have a mentor. No one volunteered and no one told me that a mentor was an essential part of building a successful career. This was one of my errors, thinking that I could manage without help, assuming I knew where to look for it. Having made this mistake, I have gone out of my way to help others avoid it and have acted and continue to act as a mentor to young and less-young attorneys, many of whom I have met through the ABA International Section of Law.

As a mentor, I have listened to horror stories of gender discrimination against women attorneys, rewritten résumés of friends who wanted to change directions, given doses of reality to Americans who want to practice law in Paris, given advice on how to request and get an increase in remuneration, and distributed networking information over many lunches in Paris. Of course, it helps to live in Paris since at least you eat and drink well while dispensing advice.

I cannot underline the necessity of finding a mentor more. Irrespective of where you are working and what you are doing, find a mentor. A mentor is someone who will help you read and interpret situations and help you keep out of trouble. He or she should be someone you respect who is willing to listen to you and keep your confidences. It's a two-way street: a good mentor is only as good as you allow that person to be. Shop around: Good mentors are not on every doorstep. A few are better than none.

The mentor can be in the organization/company/law firm where you work or outside of it. One excellent place to find supportive mentors is in the ABA, and in particular the International Section, if you are interested in international law. Other types of local, state, and specialized bar associations are also good places to start. If you are in a foreign culture, this can be more daunting, because most cultures are less transparent, frank, and open than American culture. You can always begin with the American associations in the country where you are residing, including the ABA, as a first step, and then branch out once you understand who the players are.

Never, ever (repeat this daily) make an enemy if you can avoid it. The world is a small place, and the international legal community is even smaller. I have come across acquaintances who I did not particularly take to when I first met them in Paris 28 years ago, but with whom I became friends and colleagues years thereafter and with whom I now happily share advice and information.

4.   Take What Comes Your Way and Use the Experience to Your Benefit

Unless you can see into the future (in which case, you have no business being a lawyer), you will not be able to plan your career 25 years in advance, even if you try. Life is unpredictable, and those who are successful are usually those who know how to make lemonade out of lemons. There is no right career path, and there are rarely any wrong moves. Learn from your mistakes and keep learning.

5.   Certain Truths Remain Constant

Take your studies seriously. It is easier to get a solid education when you are young than when you are 50. If you do not learn the trade well, you will not succeed, irrespective of the area of the law you intend to practice. The courses that you choose to take in law school should interest you, and you should study hard and learn the skills of a good lawyer: listening, researching, paying attention to detail, writing, and advocating.

Be curious and ask questions. The most intelligent attorneys I know are aware of what they don't know and ask questions. Don't be embarrassed or afraid. You are not expected to know all of the answers, but you are expected to know where and how to find the answers. Be wary of those who claim to know it all.

Only idiots do not or cannot change their minds. If you have made a choice that is not right for you, don't get stuck and don't be stubborn and remorseful; change directions. And while you are digesting this advice . . .

Do not be negative or complain too loudly. No matter how much you dislike what you are doing, or regret doing it, do not *ever* admit it to anyone other than your closest friends. No one likes someone who whines. The example I like to use to illustrate this point is one of my good friends who could crawl through a field of cow dung while being eaten alive by mosquitos and regale you with tales of the view and how wonderful it is. As long as you are not fooling yourself, a positive attitude about your current situation will keep your spirits bright and give you the motivation to change.

It is easier to downgrade than upgrade. It is easier to go from a big, well-known firm to a small firm than the inverse. When in doubt, start big and downsize. You do not have to stay big for more than a couple of years, but the experience is great, and it will solidify your credentials.

It is easier to make a career move if your contact book is up-to-date. Keep in contact with old and new acquaintances, friends, and mentors that you have made in the associations and organizations you have joined. This is a full-time job, and it requires attention and work. Do not neglect the benefit of keeping in touch.

It is easier and more practical to get diverse experience at the beginning of your career. Try to get as much different experience as you can in the first three to five years of your career by, for example, rotating departments in the same firm. Realizing after 25 years of real estate practice that you would rather be doing mergers and acquisitions in Italy is good—better late than never—but it is more complicated. By experiencing different types of law and different types of practices, you will learn what you do and do not like in a constructive manner instead of waking up one day and feeling like you have wasted half of your career.

6.   Travel and Learn about Different Cultures and Languages

There is nothing more embarrassing and less constructive than American attorneys who deal with non-Americans and who assume that their foreign colleagues, clients, and adversaries speak and write in "their" English; eat, drink, and dress in the same manner; and negotiate, draft and sign contracts and agreements, hire and fire employees, litigate, arbitrate and mediate, and purchase, lease, and sell assets and shares of companies and their goods and services in the same manner as they do.

It might sound trite, but any lawyer practicing in the international arena must have some sensitivity to different cultures and languages. Yes, it is helpful to learn a second and third language, if for no other reason than understanding what it means not to understand and to feel vulnerable and somewhat helpless. It is a well-earned lesson in humility, which is necessary when traveling and negotiating in languages and cultures other than the one in which we were brought up. And this advice includes the United Kingdom, Australia, Canada, and other English-speaking countries.

Verbal communication and body language is crucial. Assume you know nothing about the foreign culture, even if you think you do. A little knowledge can be dangerous, both personally and professionally. Read as much as you can, including novels by national authors, and ask as many questions as you feel is appropriate. Blissful ignorance does not exist in international law. Living and working outside the United States in whatever capacity is always a fruitful experience. My credo is: "Look, listen, and learn."

I.   Conclusion

I have attempted to share my insights into my own career and draw certain conclusions from them, which I hope will be useful to you. Undoubtedly, you will have your own experiences and will draw your own conclusions

There are many things I wish I had known before I started my career: I wish I had known that I needed a mentor; I wish someone had told me that networking is essential; I wish I had joined the International Section of the ABA before I turned 40. And I wish I had been able to read this book!

Know that there is no secret gate or password to become an international lawyer. Become a good lawyer first, and focus on what interests you. Maintain an open mind about job opportunities, know yourself, and keep a sense of humor and perspective about your life and career. The rest is, as we used to say, "a piece of cake"!

What You Find Out After You Find Ice

3

by Bruce Horowitz

Many years later, as he faced the firing squad, Colonel Aureliano Buendía would remember that afternoon long ago when his father took him to discover ice for the first time.[1]

A.   Finding Ice

Ice led me to a career in international law and to living in Ecuador. Not the magical ice at the beginning of *One Hundred Years of Solitude*, but rather a more mundane specimen found at motels everywhere in

---

[1] The first sentence in Gabriel García Márquez's *One Hundred Years of Solitude* (1967). In the original, "Muchos años después, frente al pelotón de fusilamiento, el coronel Aureliano Buendía había de recordar aquella tarde remota en que su padre lo llevó a conocer el hielo."

the United States in the summer of 1969—45 days and counting down to a concert that was about to lift off from Woodstock, New York.

My particular career-defining piece of ice was waiting for me in a large, metal bin located under the outside staircase next to the parking lot at a motel in northern Alabama. I wasn't staying at that motel. We were traveling in a 1960 Plymouth with a nickname but no personality, driving across the country—away from what would be Woodstock, if the truth be told. We slept in a tent, not in motels. Motels were important to us that summer at the hot end of the 1960s, because motels in the South had swimming pools that seemed to be open to the car-driving public, and because all motels in the South had their ice machines outside under the stairs.

Yes, stolen motel ice was at the lip of the slope that drew me into a life of international law and a career in the tropics. And no, I was not caught cold-fingered by the Alabama State Troopers, nor have I been hiding out in the Andes ever since. Rather, a nameless stranger in front of me at that particular ice machine, while filling his own ice chest, saw our car's northern plates and asked where we were headed. "Out West," I said. "You?" "Peace Corps, Brazil," the stranger replied. And then he packed off his ice chest and headed east.

Back in 1960, when I was eleven, I read an article written by a U.S. Senator about his plan (were he to be elected) to train and send young people to foreign countries to work for peace and to help improve the lives of poor people. It was a thrilling concept. I was a young person, and this was for me. But young for the Senator meant at least 18, and I was not that old yet.

"Peace Corps, Brazil," the stranger had replied before he got into his car and drove east. Here I was now at 20, in the midst of reading George Orwell's *Homage to Catalonia*, wanting to be in any foreign country other than Vietnam, and wanting to help people. By the time I got back to the Plymouth with that afternoon's stolen ice, and with a thunderstorm galloping toward us from the northwest, I had begun looking for a local library where I could spin a globe, close my eyes, and put my finger down on . . . Canada. Of course, at that time, if you wanted to serve in the Peace

Corps, you had to sit down, rather than stand up beside the spinning globe—then you could close your eyes, and put your finger down on . . . Ecuador.

A few weeks later, a human being bounced out onto the surface of the Moon, under the light of which in the Grand Tetons I was mapping my future—and it was Ecuador. My senior year would no longer be dedicated to the English Country Aristocracy Honors History Project. Instead, that dedication would careen toward Ecuador Area Studies, the Economics of Development, the Politics of Under-development, away from French and onto Spanish, Latin-American history, South American art, archaeology, and anthropology—and international law, for reasons beyond my control, as explained next.

B. Finding the Law

I was only 18 months old when I almost discovered a lawyer for the first time. I had somehow squeezed through the slats in our picket fence. When my mother could not find me in the backyard, she ran out the front door, and the first person she saw was our neighbor across the street sitting on his porch in his wicker rocker behind the pages of the afternoon newspaper. This neighbor was a lawyer and our town's own State Legislative Representative. After considering my mother's question as to whether he had seen her infant son anywhere, he folded back the top half of the newspaper, and pointed his pipe in the direction toward where he had seen me headed, given the time that had passed, and my forward momentum when he had first observed me waddling down the middle of Walker Street past his front porch.

The only other thing I knew about the lawyers in my town before I turned 16 was that one hunted squirrels and the other one lived with two Doberman Pinschers and hunted ducks. It was right after I turned 16 that I met the first lawyer whom I connected with the law, at the point when he was telling my family that we had nothing to worry about because my father had left the family's finances in good order. Thus was I introduced to the law. This lawyer was clear-headed and a good person, and he spurred my interest in the law by taking down from his own library a well-read copy of Justice Holmes' *The Common Law*, and placing it into my hands.

From then until law school, the only other lawyers I met on a professional basis were two draft counselors, who scared the crap out of me vis-à-vis the long arm and the mailed fist of the U.S. Selective Service System in reference to my low draft lottery number. It happened in my senior year, following directly upon my internationalist conversion by motel ice. So, in addition to learning about everything Hispanic American that last year of college, I had taken up the self-guided (no-credit) study of the Selective Service (military draft) laws, where I suddenly fell or emerged into that tangential legal anti-universe dealing with the negative status and lack of rights of Stateless Persons. Although this was but one small step into international law, it was like starting my legal career as the clam rather than the pearl diver. For someone who was just then traversing without a guide rope over page 95 of Jean-Paul Sartre's *Being and Nothingness*, "statelessness" was the perfect place to plant my flag on the mountain of international law.

C. Finding Peace

Three years have now passed. I am walking by myself through a swamp in the Ecuadorian Amazon Basin, wearing a red bandana and carrying a surveyor's transit, going into my fourth year as a volunteer surveyor in Ecuador. I have been lost in this section of Heaven for going on 10 hours now. The sun is sinking quickly, as it always does in a rainforest on the equator.

I find a trail just after dusk, and when I get back to my village a few days later, there is a letter waiting from New York University (NYU) Law School. I had advised them that I would be staying in the Peace Corps another year and had asked them to hold my admission for just one more year. The letter from NYU advised me that it was to be now or never.

My time in the Peace Corps was an extraordinarily enriching part of my life, but it is almost all beyond the scope of an essay about why I got into international law. However, my experience there repeatedly told me that I could better serve as a lawyer, and after every new survey trek, my knees supported that conclusion. More importantly, an Ecuadorian friend of mine was about to become the first of his people to attend law school. Our plan was to work together after we had both graduated from law school.

Why had I chosen NYU? Because it was in the same city as the United Nations. During my three years at NYU Law School, I never set foot inside the United Nations or even checked to see what subway line to take to get to the UN Plaza. For some of us, the reasons why we start something have nothing to do with why we stay. I had chosen my college for a silly reason, but I stayed there because it (Brandeis University) was an amazing center of learning and social commitment. I chose Ecuador because it had mountains and was, I thought, small enough to learn all about in a senior year. I stayed there because it really was better than Woodstock and a walk on the Moon all put together, and because the people kept trying to teach me about wisdom, honesty, courage, beauty, and kindness.

I went to NYU Law School because of the UN, and stayed because NYU happened to be a factory that magically turned out handcrafted lawyers. I went to Alaska for a summer law clerkship, and stayed for nine years because of the high-quality and goodwill of the lawyers and judges, and because where else could a lawyer stand by his unwavering client over a hole in the ice a mile from land waiting for dinner to surface, and expecting any minute to turn into another chunk of ice himself. Twenty-two years ago, I returned to Ecuador for love. I have stayed in Ecuador for love, and because no one has ordered me to leave, yet.

During the Vietnam War, there was a slogan commonly used against the anti-war movement that went, "America, love it or leave it!" The U.S. Peace Corps later untwisted that phrase into a very successful recruiting campaign called "America, love it AND leave it."

D.   Finding a Peaceful Place to Practice Law

Although it would surprise most U.S. citizens, many Latin-American immigrants migrate to places other than the United States. While most diplomats may have their hearts set on Paris, London, or

Washington, D.C., lawyers who dream about living abroad, like other immigrants without a safety net, tend to be more open-minded, and find themselves traveling to and sometimes putting down roots in unlikely places.

I would venture a guess that most lawyers who move to other countries expect to return home within a few years. Their expectation is to learn things that will help them professionally upon their return home, and they may hope to make some money in the meantime. Most of them learn a lot, and some make some money during the learning process. A few of them become trans-national practitioners. A few stay.

For some years now, the internationalization of the law and the cross-border harmonization of the laws have been galloping full abreast to catch up with the globalization of the economy. Ignoring for the moment the issue of host-country lawyer back-lash, it is becoming easier for foreign lawyers to work and stay, and sometimes even practice law.

Of the fifteen or so foreign lawyers I know who have stayed to live in Ecuador, about half of them (evenly divided between male and female lawyers) have married Ecuadorians, or have long-term relationships with Ecuadorians, or have long-term expectations for many short-term relationships with Ecuadorians.

Only a few of the lawyers who do not arrive in-country through an Embassy, a nongovernmental organization (NGO), or a transnational corporation find work as lawyers or as foreign legal consultants. Some of those who come down freelance get into the in-country legal field after starting out in administration, or as legal translators, or both. In the United States, I worked for the Legal Services Corporation (or what the English used to call "the poor man's lawyer"), in both litigation and law-office man-agement, first in Alaska and then, for the last two years before I returned to Ecuador, back in my home state of Ohio. For the first four years after returning to Ecuador, I taught Philosophy, Logic, and Economics and learned quite a bit about Philosophy and Logic; I also learned that being a good lawyer is easier, so much easier, than being a good teacher.

With another child on the way, I decided to return to the law, and while litigation was out for an unlicensed lawyer in Ecuador, I found a good firm that was interested in my management experience, combined with their hope that—as flatly translated from the Spanish legal phrase—I would be "intelligent in English." I had also come through the door with a decade worth of useful practice in contracts, persuasive argument, negotiations, and some understanding of the U.S. legal system. I was found to be of some use, in a generalized way, when Ecuadorian clients of the firm needed initial guidance on a broad expanse of U.S. legal matters. I became a good legal translator. I was introduced to intellectual property law at the local and international level with kind help from many local lawyers, to whom I shall be forever grateful. I also learned that one needs all five or six years of law school to prepare a simple, valid civil law Power of Attorney.

Today, in addition to law office management, my practice involves international intellectual property, litigation risk and settlement analysis, international employment, agency and distributorship matters, and anti-corruption compliance and anti-public extortion work and training for individual clients and corporate client groups.

E. Finding Your Own Path

Walking out of law school and into a foreign country where the people speak your language but have a different legal system will allow you to take a job as a legal messenger. Walking out of law school and into a foreign country where you speak their language will allow you to take a job as a translator. Walking into another country with a license to practice from back home, experience in at least one foreign language, and at least two or three years of experience in contracts, international trade, corporate law, accounting, American Depositary Receipts (ADRs), and negotiations will give you a boost when you go overseas to look for work with a foreign law firm. Having a similar background, but in the areas of litigation, health law, human rights, environmental, employment law, and community development will give you a boost when you go overseas to work for a foreign or international NGO.

One interesting thing about living in a different legal culture is that one day you will truly understand that your legal system and their legal system have nothing in common; the next day you will truly understand that there is really no difference. Another interesting thing about all legal cultures is that each one has developed special overly long and ungrammatical incantations, which are fun to repeat, and which magically cause your nose to rise slightly and your lips to purse, and cause you to feel at least two centimeters taller.

On the other hand, unless you are Marcel Marceau, Charlie Chaplin, or Mario Moreno, the first thing you lose and the last thing you get back when you live in a new language is your sense of humor, even when you thought you never had one. It feels life-threatening when you are standing around in a circle with your newfound friends, while one of them is telling a joke, and when the punch line comes, you have an out-of-body experience seeing everyone else laughing and looking at you, while you display what is called a grimace. You begin to wish that jokes would never start, and if they start, would never end.

Do not be discouraged; your sense of humor will return in five or six years, although during that time your misunderstood reactions to misunderstood punch lines will make you seem to those around you as hypocritical, shallow, haughty, or distraught. Finally, the day will come when you can actually say something funny, intentionally funny. Then, after those five years of being laughed at, you will actually be laughed with, and at. You will have arrived. Humility and patience are good for a lawyer, as they are for anyone with some degree of power.

My Career as a Latin-American Transactional Lawyer

4

by Andrew J. Markus

A. Introduction

As I approach my 25th year in the practice of law in law firms, I can now reflect on what it is to be an international lawyer, and particularly one focused on mergers and acquisitions and other transactions in Latin America. I wrote a chapter, "Miami International Practice," for the first edition of *Careers in International Law* in 1993. Looking back at that chapter, it appears to me that many of my reflections are still valid and appropriate. However, I have quite a different perspective on the practice of law, given the great advances in technology that have occurred in the past 15 years. I would therefore like to relate how I became an international lawyer, what it is like to practice law in a law firm, what it is like to undertake Latin-American mergers and acquisitions, and what you can do to pursue a career in international law.

B.   Why I Became an International Lawyer

I became a lawyer, naturally enough, because I had an early interest in the law. I remember reading a book, *So You Want to Be a
Lawyer*, when I was in seventh grade. Whatever that book said
to me, it must have been powerful, because here I am, all these
years later, a practicing lawyer. To be fair, my father also helped
me become the business lawyer I am today. He was a businessperson and exposed me to a wide variety of U.S. businesses. After
that, I knew that the only kind of lawyer I wanted to be was a
business lawyer.

So why did I then become an international business lawyer?
Sometimes—and I think this happens more often than not—people
find their special talents by accident. That was certainly what happened to me. My special talent is an ability to relate to things international. I became aware that I had a natural affinity toward the
cultural aspects of international matters and that I related well to
individuals from other cultures as a result of my travels in Europe
in the summer of 1970. Travel was an eye-opening experience for
me. I knew then that I was born to be international. I was going
to law school. So I aimed to make myself an international lawyer.
Little did I appreciate the long and interesting path I had chosen.

C.   Law Firm Practice

How does talking about what it is like to practice in a law firm
pertain to your path to international law practice? Well, let's
assume that you are at the beginning, or nearly the beginning, of
your career path as you read this chapter. As important as knowing that you want to do something international in the law is the
environment from which you attempt to do it. This is important
for several reasons:

- As a lawyer, you will be hired by a client for your legal
  skills. If you do not have top-of-the-line training, it is just
  that much harder to be a good lawyer. It will not serve

you well to be a culturally aware lawyer if you cannot lawyer your way out of a paper bag.

- It is always easier to swim downstream. If you are fortunate enough to be hired and trained by a great law firm,
you will have many more options in the future than if you
start by hanging out your own shingle.

- If you practice law in an environment in which anything
international is met with incomprehension, your international aspirations will wither and die unless you change to
an environment that is supportive.

What big firms generally offer that small firms do not is the
luxury of training and the opportunity to work on large transactions. You may not feel that this is a luxury at 11 p.m., while you
work on reviewing due diligence or drafting an agreement for the
client to review the next morning, but you will find, in hindsight,
that you have learned much and, in fact, have an edge on most
of your contemporaries. Large transactions bring into play all the
skills that are required to do smaller transactions properly, but
your firm can bill for these services and therefore has the luxury
of allowing you to be on the team.

To be hired by a large, prestigious law firm in the United
States, you must apply for and be accepted to do a summer clerkship at the firm. The lesson here is: plan early. Many a second-
or third-year law student has approached me in January or later
about becoming an associate in my firm. Invariably, they have
been too late. With some foresight, that tardy law student could
have been taking his or her place in the class of associates from
which tomorrow's best international lawyers will come.

What small firms offer that big firms do not is hands-on experience at an early age. However seductive this may be, delay this
gratification until you have received a good grounding in your
chosen discipline. While there are exceptions, small firms often
do not provide a viable platform for high-level international corporate work. On the other hand, small firms do provide a lawyer
with the ability to handle a client's transaction from beginning to
end and to be responsible for it. They also provide young lawyers

with the opportunity (a mixed blessing, to be sure) to generate their own clients.

Medium-size firms (by that I mean firms with 20 to 100 lawyers) seem to have the disadvantages of both large and small firms. The medium-size firm often does not provide hands-on experience at an early age or a viable platform for high-level international corporate work. It also does not provide a young lawyer with the opportunity to generate his or her own business. The trend appears to be toward larger sized firms, and even firms that would qualify in my numbering system as large (those with more than 100 to about 400 lawyers) are dissolving or being acquired at an accelerating rate. Thus, in the future, it may be that there are two types of law firms—the mega firm and the small boutique firm.

D. What Does a Latin-American Transactional Lawyer Do?

My son has asked me what I do all day. Do I buy and sell Latin-American companies? Sometimes, either directly or indirectly. Do I practice foreign (non-U.S.) law? No. Most often, I am engaged in the practice of U.S. law with non-U.S. aspects. For instance, if I am engaged in an asset acquisition in which many of the assets are non-U.S. companies or operations, many issues arise under foreign law. The framework of my agreement, however, is U.S. (typically New York or Delaware) law. The entities involved are typically New York or Delaware corporations or other entities. Therefore, for instance, if some of the assets are in a Brazilian *limitada*, questions as to title to the assets, rights attributable to the assets, and the like are certainly governed by Brazilian law. Do I opine as to these aspects? No. Local counsel is an absolute necessity in this circumstance and plays a key role in the validity of such an acquisition.

If, on the other hand, I am engaged in a merger, it is generally of U.S. entities with operations in Latin America. In this type of transaction, usually many more issues of U.S. law present themselves than issues of foreign law. One thing is virtually certain: the U.S. entities' operations will be accomplished by a number of Latin-

American entities. However, the transaction is rarely positioned so that mergers between the in-country entities form the transaction. Generally, the transaction takes place at a level in which defined commercial law, such as that of New York or Delaware, may govern and in which the courts of New York or Delaware or an international arbitral tribunal can have jurisdiction. Thus, once again I am a U.S. lawyer practicing U.S. law with international aspects.

E. How You Can Pursue a Career in International Law

My thoughts on this matter are strictly U.S.-oriented. I have practiced in large and small firms, in my own firms, in other people's self-made firms, and in old established firms. Whatever else they have in common, for an international lawyer, the environment of the firm is the most important thing to consider. If the firm does not have a commitment to international practice, spend your time getting the best domestic law education you can and plan to move in a few years when you have a good, basic knowledge of what it is like to be a first-class lawyer.

Another aspect to consider on the path to "internationaldom" is that law firms are, at their essence, businesses. The exigencies of businesses often demand that their employees take paths different from those envisioned by them or the firm. This realization came to me one day when, having been hired to do international things in a law firm, I found myself doing real estate finance and development work instead. It was not what I was suited to do. It was not what I had planned to do. It was not even what my law firm had planned that I do. But it was what there was to do. I used the experience to make myself a more well-rounded lawyer, but I never forgot what I wanted to do with my career.

As it became apparent that my international opportunity was not going to occur in that firm, I did what is now commonplace—I changed firms. I did not move to a new firm for the money. My inducement was that the new opportunity would bring me closer to my career goal. That framework for viewing my career has led me to make several more changes in my career path. I practice now in Miami as the chair of the International Practice Group of one of the largest and best regarded Florida law firms doing corporate work, such as mergers and acquisitions for Latin Americans and Europeans in the United States and for U.S. and non-U.S. companies in Latin America.

I have learned three important lessons:

1. *Be clear about what you want to do.* Try to really feel certain internally and try not to fool yourself about your desires. You may find that you really don't want to be a lawyer at all, but a businessperson, an artist, or a writer. Or maybe (God forbid) you want to be a trial lawyer. One thing is evident to me: If you aren't clear with yourself, you will find yourself moving in directions that you don't understand.

2. *Use what you learn, wherever and however you learn it, to further your chosen direction.* I could have been a real estate lawyer representing large institutions in complex real estate lending transactions or representing developers building large projects. Instead, in my early career, I took my good domestic law skills and applied them to representing non-U.S. investors and financiers of real estate projects. From there I developed relationships and gained experience in the transactional aspects of business representation. My clients started doing things other than real estate or introduced me to others who did things other than real estate. I factored all of these learning elements into my chosen direction and eventually began to do complex mergers and acquisitions domestically and internationally.

3. *Develop relationships early and often.* I have heard it said that the seeds for business one plants as a lawyer often take a long time to germinate. What is true is that your friends will be the ones to send you business and help you develop future contacts. As a young lawyer, your friends will generally not be in a position to help you (or you, them) at the start. Be patient and keep contact with your friends. They are your future.

Finally, do not despair if the job that you find initially does not appear to be international in scope. Just remember to keep focused on what you want to do as you go along and look for an opportunity to do it. Keep your eye on where you want to go and not where you are coming from. Assuming you still want to be an international lawyer, move in that direction. I do not think it is heresy anymore to suggest that you may need to move from one firm to several different firms before you feel that you are doing what you want to do. You might not make it on your first, second, or even third move, but keep your eye on what you want, and you will achieve it.

A Foreign (to the U.S.) Viewpoint on Practicing International Law

5

by Marcelo Bombau

A. Introduction

I have no doubt that U.S. attorneys and U.S.-trained attorneys are in the right place to practice international law. I state this because the world outside the United States generally looks to and follows U.S. trends, legal practice, and jurisprudence. Likewise, and in my opinion, of all the countries and economies of the world, the United States is the most international of all. Therefore, U.S. legal practice is, by nature or by its adoption by foreign countries, the most international career of all.

Although there are different ways of getting involved in international legal practice, together with the certainty that there are no road maps, it is equally true that many starting points do, in fact, exist. In this chapter, I will share my experience of how I got involved in international legal practice and give you my suggestions on how to approach said practice and best abide by its (unwritten) rules.

B.   How It All Began

The majority of colleagues with whom I have spoken over the years agree with me in asserting that their involvement in international law did not occur overnight, and that many times they have had to change directions. My reality does not differ from theirs: I have had different experiences on my path to a full-fledged international practice.

I was probably influenced by my father and by the illusion that ambassadors lived a great life. I had always envisioned myself as part of the Argentine Foreign Affairs department. That is why I took all of the internationally related subjects at law school very seriously. However, one day, after speaking with another ambassador, I awoke from the dreamed lifestyle and suddenly found myself more interested in private international law rather than public international law.

I began my legal practice at an international, well-respected firm, where I have practiced for the last 25 years. This stability has been very helpful in that there was an international atmosphere in this firm, which assisted my goal in becoming an international practitioner. Although my practice has evolved over the years in different directions—from being a labor law attorney to a commercial litigator—I have always tried to be as close to international legal issues as possible. In fact, I am now a mergers and acquisitions (M&A) attorney who is actively involved in an international practice. Quite often, your practice is client-driven, and my experience is a confirmation of how client-driven needs change the course of one's personal history.

In my case, a U.S. multinational was in the process of acquiring a large company in Argentina, which was owned by a local businessperson. I had been hired to do the legal due diligence by U.S.-lead counsel of the U.S. multinational. After months of preliminary talks, the U.S.-lead counsel presented the local businessperson with sizable drafts of stock purchase and shareholder's agreements in English. The local businessperson promptly asked where the Spanish versions were, to which the U.S.-lead counsel conclusively stated that "95 percent of international deals are done in English." The local businessperson replied that his deal would then fall within the remaining 5 percent.

The next morning I received a call from the general counsel of the client, the U.S. multinational, who indicated that I would be leading all of the negotiations and drafting sessions going forward because, otherwise, the seller would simply walk away from the deal, having demanded—effective immediately—that the U.S.-lead counsel be removed from the deal. This is how I got fully involved in all of the international aspects of an M&A transaction.

I continued to represent this client after the first deal closed and in such capacity have traveled throughout Latin America doing deals and trying to close the cultural gaps between Anglo and Latin ways of seeing things and doing business. Thus, the wrong answer given by the U.S. attorney and the subsequent regional legal needs of my client positioned me into the international arena. Because I did not want to run the fate of the U.S.-lead attorney who had been removed from the deal, I started thinking of suggestions and tips for an international practitioner, which I would like to share. At least up until now, they have been very helpful to me and have been my guidelines in the international law arena.

C. Suggestions and Tips

In no specific order, here are several suggestions, which I recommend to any lawyer who wants to enter and stay involved in international legal practice:

1. *Choose a type of practice.* Be it private, in-house, or governmental, choose one that is coherent with your personal goals.

2. *Develop an expertise as much as possible.* Choose and specialize in a geographic region or a particular area of law, such as antitrust, tax, M&A, environmental.

3. *Start as young as possible.* You might have to change courses more than once, but stay on your own path.

4. *Be the best lawyer you can be.* An international attorney is often a generalist and a specialist, and his or her client usually presumes that he or she knows almost everything.

5. *Join international organizations.* Contact U.S. embassies abroad and become active in associations such as the Section of International Law of the ABA, business communities, and Chambers of Commerce.

6. *Learn about different cultures.* Respectfully said, this is one of the most vital points yet the most difficult to achieve for U.S. attorneys. Japanese, Argentine, U.S., and Swedish cultures, for example, differ enormously. You would be surprised to know how much I gained professionally with some U.S. clients simply by knowing how certain NFL teams had done on a given weekend!

7. *Find persons you are able to trust both personally and professionally.* Having reliable international contacts will allow you to become known within your firm and by your clients as the go-to person.

8. *Learn legal principles.* Countries around the world are ruled by very clear legal principles. Try to learn those broad principles.

9. *Learn the language.* Although this is not an absolute must from my point of view, being able to speak more than one language, even with difficulties, will improve the rapport on both sides of the transaction.

10. *Keep up with the major events of the foreign country or region.* Presidential elections, economic booms, and thriving fields of business—I have come across many U.S. attorneys who have taken this point seriously and who have acquired an admirable knowledge of local events. Do the same.

11. *Make people feel that you are an equal.* Strange as an issue may seem, do not overreact or seem surprised when hearing the way legal business works in a different country. Show that you are trying to understand concepts that may differ substantially from U.S. practices.

12. *Increase your international contacts.* A good and reliable database takes years to build. Once you've built one, keep in touch with your contacts. Having good and reliable international contacts allows not only the saving of time but also the tranquility of having reached or contacted someone truly reliable.

13. *Write articles in international publications.* Do not rule out writing joint articles with foreign lawyers.

The road to becoming an international attorney may seem endless and unclear, but at least in my case, the path in and of itself is truly rewarding.

Part 2

Private Sector

A Solo Practitioner's Pathway to International Law Practice

by Aaron Schildhaus

6

A. Introduction

People have asked how someone born in a small town in Vermont, who had never traveled outside North America, would have a passion for international law. Either I was born too soon or international law became popular too late. I was passionately interested in the concept, but rather frustrated by the reality. For example, when I went to law school, I took a one-semester elective entitled "International and Comparative Law." It was the *only* course on international law that was offered. Today, my law school prides itself on having one of the richest curricula in the field of international law. It now lists more than 100 courses on international law and offers JD and LLM degrees in six countries outside the United States.

How did I, a solo practitioner, end up in the field of international law?

When Lyndon Johnson was President, he scolded Americans into seeing their own country first before venturing abroad to see others. I had taken his advice and had seen quite a few states, all of which seemed more or less similar, which is no surprise if driving across the country on interstate highways is any test. After heeding the words of LBJ, I still felt there must be something of interest outside the United States, so in the summer before my last year of law school, I ventured outside North America for the first time. All summer long, I traveled around Europe. It was an eye-opener, and I haven't closed my eyes or ears since. I was determined to be an international lawyer, whatever that meant.

The following spring, my law school published a "Placement Publication," which had all of the graduating seniors' pictures with categories of information filled in by each of us. Among the categories was: "Type of practice sought." I listed "International Law (Commercial Aspects)." Another category was "Location Preferred." My entry: "Abroad." In those days, that was considered very funny. I remember people pointing at me and laughing: "International Law . . . Abroad . . . ha, ha, ha." In fact, I had the last laugh. I have been practicing international law now for more than 30 years.

B.   Entering the Field of International Law

Finding a job in international law was a major challenge in the early 1970s, given that so few professionals recognized it as a separate practice area. My first job after graduation was with a law firm in Washington, D.C., where I was assigned to help draft and codify municipal legislation that could be standardized for computer applications; those were the very, very early days of computer use by lawyers. After I passed the D.C. Bar, I found employment in Boston as a staff attorney in the legal department of an insurance company with home offices in the United Kingdom. Other than the fact that I occasionally met a chap with a British accent, there was not too much international law there, either.

Like many others now in the field, my first jobs were not international. But I was determined to put my legal training to work in a productive way that would expose me to a broader world—one that would not end at the shores of the Atlantic or Pacific oceans. In my mind, the practice of international law was something that could not be done effectively unless one had the chance to live and experience different legal systems, different cultures, and different languages. Thus, as I honed my basic legal skills with increasing frustration at the lack of any international connection, I took whatever money I had and traveled across the Atlantic. However, employers could not understand anyone not working 50 weeks a year and untold hours per week. Travel was expensive, time was short, and jobs were on the line. Wherever I worked, I kept seeking the international exposure and the right angle to get me into the field.

Luck always plays its part. It is often said that if you try hard enough and long enough, you can create your own luck. It is probably more accurate to state that if you look around intelligently and put yourself in the right places, chance may bring an opportunity to your door. The difficulty lies in spotting the opportunity for what it is and persevering to turn that chance into a lucky break. My chance came when I was hired as an in-house lawyer by PepsiCo, Inc. in its leasing and financing division. Thanks to the mentoring of my immediate boss, I learned the nuts and bolts of drafting complex financial and corporate transactions, the niceties of understanding otherwise abstruse provisions of contracts, and the process of properly shepherding closing documentation. This experience enabled me to appreciate the wordsmithing we lawyers do, despite its often pejorative connotation.

I learned to be precise, because the discipline of precision spills over into an ability to cut through linguistic and cultural differences in order to express oneself accurately and be clearly understood by others. Later, when learning and working in foreign languages, this skill became paramount in my arsenal of legal tools. It remains so to this day, and I remain grateful to my boss and mentor for insisting on the highest standards in the analysis of transactions and the drafting abilities I put into practice in order to complete the deals.

Although I handled a few deals involving offshore issues and parties, I was still hungry for far more international work, and PepsiCo. proved to be a major stepping stone to my career: It had an excellent law department and a terrific and supportive general counsel. When I expressed my interest in going to Europe, I was not discouraged. To the contrary, the company reimbursed me for the cost of my first French language lessons. And so, with the blessing of my general counsel, I was granted a sabbatical, which has now lasted since 1975.

C. My Move Abroad

I decided to move to Paris, where I was certain I would be greeted with open arms and many job offers. My theory about moving to Paris then was simple. If a firm did not have to pay my moving costs and cost-of-living, it would—so I assumed and hoped—jump at the chance to employ me as a local hire.

I arrived in Paris in the summer of 1975, the time of year when everyone thinks of summer holiday, not summer hiring. However, in September, Paris was transformed into a beehive of activity. Shortly thereafter, I landed a job with a Franco-German law firm that was a spin-off of the largest French firm at the time. It was a bit of a fluke, because the senior partner of the firm wanted a native-speaking American lawyer who could speak German and lived in Paris. Although it was perfect for me, it soon became obvious that neither my German nor my French were at the necessary levels. I rose to the challenge, steadily improved my German and my French, and began to cope with all of the challenges of integrating myself into a new and very different culture. I was assigned, almost immediately, to work on a global acquisition project for a major Canadian multinational.

After about a year, my youth, my optimism, and the excitement of Paris propelled me to leave the security of the law firm and to strike out on my own. Unfortunately, I did this much too soon, as I was too young and inexperienced, and consequently seriously unprepared for such a venture. The following years had many ups and downs. It is true that I learned by doing, but it is worth pointing out that the school of hard knocks has classrooms all around the globe, even in the City of Light. However, despite the hard times, there were many kind, helping hands along the way. An American lawyer, in-house general counsel with a major international oil company, gave me corporate work and became a good friend; a German lawyer gave me legal consultation work involving U.S. law and became a lifelong friend; a Paris law firm with a conflict referred to me a fascinating U.S. litigation case with multicountry parties, requiring me to conduct discovery in France; and a U.S. lawyer with a major Wall Street firm's Paris office let me use the office to receive clients. Many others, mostly Parisians, went out of their way to help me.

Surviving as a solo practitioner in Paris is not one of the easiest things to do, and I would not recommend it to the faint of heart. Not that I was particularly strong-hearted; I just did not know any better. Nevertheless, by targeted networking, I managed to get some major but mostly minor European companies as clients for outbound business to the United States. Unfortunately, without an American law firm supporting my efforts, the clients all ended up, quite naturally, with the American law firms that were handling their business in the United States. This was a good example of lawyering one's way out of business.

D. Returning to the United States and Joining the Section of International Law

In 1986, I returned to Washington, D.C., with no idea where to begin, as I had lost most of my prior contacts. Nevertheless, I had decided that I had the right skills to be a great international lawyer, and I was determined to succeed in international law from a base in the United States. I was not interested in any other kind of law. I figured, at that stage in my life, that if I were to take a job dealing solely with domestic legal issues, I would never be able to get off that treadmill. How does a now middle-aged solo practitioner without business compete as an international lawyer in the international capital of the world? How could I get business, and how could I meet the right people with whom to network?

I was told by a lawyer I met in the process of knocking on doors in Washington, D.C., that the best way to network was to get active in the right organization. I will never forget this advice. Within months of returning to the United States, I attended an ABA annual meeting in New York City. As a business lawyer, I attended both the Business Law and the International Law Section programs. Very quickly, I found my new home in the International Section. The focus was global, and the members were open and friendly. Most of them shared my international interests, different language capabilities, and living experiences abroad. I joined committees, began attending meetings, and became active in the Section. It is the single most important and effective organization for practicing international lawyers in the world, and being a part of it is rewarding every day. I never looked back.

E.   My Most Gratifying Professional Experiences

Fairly quickly after joining the ABA and becoming active in the International Section, I decided to set up my own law firm, The International Business Law Firm. Joining the ABA and setting up my own international law firm are among the most gratifying things I have done. Although I eventually left the law firm I founded, I never left the Section. The more involved I became in it, the more I honed my skills as an international lawyer, due in no small part to the resources of the Section. Through its committees and members, the Section is an outstanding and accessible reservoir of exceptional legal talent.

Since joining the International Section, I have dutifully attended the Council meetings, where the major international issues are discussed and debated. Now I am a member of the Council and am honored to sit at the same table with so many accomplished and expert international lawyers. I still attend as many substantive programs at meetings as possible, which allows me to remain on the cutting edge of international legal issues and developments and to gain the perspectives of the experts who participate in the panels and on the scores of committees in the Section.

In addition, the Section's activities outside the United States, whether ILEX trips, international bar leader trips, or fall meetings in Brussels, London, or elsewhere, always bring a special dimension to Section membership. As an inveterate traveler, I participate in these trips whenever I can, and I never regret a moment of them. They are the combination of so much that is positive in international law practice: interesting places, interesting people, current and pertinent information about major international legal issues, and most of all, a sense of continually contributing to global understanding and good relations among members of the legal profession around the world.

Through Section activities, I have become conversant in an amazing variety of international legal issues, and I have had the opportunity to meet lawyers from every branch of the profession: law professors, U.S. and other government lawyers, those working for international and multilateral organizations, in-house corporate counsels, other solo practitioners like myself, law students, and the young and the old, hailing from Africa, Latin America, Eastern and Western Europe, Asia, and the Middle East.

I have been exposed to the great legal minds of our generation: Justice Stephen Breyer, Judge Thomas Buergenthal, Harold Burman, Hans Corell, President Valery Giscard d'Estaing, Marsha Echols, Dean Claudio Grossman, John Jackson, Henry King, Dean Harold Koh, Boris Kozolchyk, Monroe Leigh, Eleanor Roberts Lewis, Ramon Mullerat, Betty Southard Murphy, Justice Sandra Day O'Connor, Peter Pfund, Ibrahim Shihata, Louis Sohn, David Stewart, K. K. Venugopal, Don Wallace, Ruth Wedgwood, and many, many others. Not only have I had the opportunity to meet these giants of the profession and been able to share their thoughts and ideas, but I have also worked with and am honored to have many of them as friends. I am very grateful to my colleagues and proud of them and their achievements.

The single proudest moment of my career was also my biggest and nicest surprise: when I received the Mayre Rasmussen award in recognition of my contributions to the advancement of women in international law. As the only male recipient of the award to date, I found myself in extraordinary company: Mayre Rasmussen, Lucinda Low, Dianna Kempe, and Rona Mears. I could only accept the award with the understanding that we have but scratched the surface. Deborah Enix-Ross, the first African-American Chair of the Section, appointed a Diversity Task Force, on which I was proud to serve. I am even prouder to be part of the leadership of the first Section in the ABA to have a Diversity Officer, who will be responsible for promoting and ensuring continued and increased tolerance of differences in race, gender, national origin, age, abilities, sexual preferences, and other types of diversity in the Section.

F. Conclusion

My career in international law started many years ago, and I hope it will live as long as I do. Every day brings new challenges, more knowledge, and new friends. I have the sense of helping to make a difference in the world by working on important policy matters in committees, on the Council, and with the larger ABA. I look forward to every day with the same great thrill I did when I first explored the profession. As I said earlier, I never looked back. There is too much to look forward to!

The Road to an International In-House Legal Career

7

by Janet Wright and Carolyn Herzog

A. Introduction

We approached writing this chapter with the knowledge that we had ended up in a similar place, having followed different paths and starting with only three key factors in common: (1) we are both women; (2) we are both lawyers; and (3) we both share an interest in international practice. Where Carolyn began as a legal generalist with subject-matter expertise and moved into more specific areas of legal expertise, Janet began her career focusing on a legal area of expertise that lent itself to a broader area of practice in support of a similar line of business. This scenario is an oversimplified view of in-house counsel, and the role of global counsel is more complex than ever before. In this chapter, we discuss not only how and why we arrived at our current roles, but also how we work to support the evolving definition of global counsel, the key factors for success, and considerations for any person contemplating a move to in-house work in an international environment.

B. How Did We Get Here and Why Do We Stay?

First and foremost, we agree that we are in our current positions because we work with great people, we have interesting challenges to tackle, our careers continue to develop, and we have a global focus that keeps us interested and engaged. What each of us does today represents an evolution from where we started—in part planned, in part as a result of a changing business environment. Being flexible and prepared to take on new challenges is important to your long-term success in an in-house environment.

Janet: I spent 10 years in law firms doing tax and corporate work, including corporate transactions, mergers and acquisitions (M&A), international tax planning, tax litigation, and partnership investments. Having spent five years each at two large law firms, I was ready for a change. I took an in-house position as tax counsel at Dell, focusing on the international tax planning for expansions in Asia and Latin America. And then I moved to a corporate counsel position and did everything from securities work to global equity compensation compliance to medical privacy compliance. Today, I lead a team of eight that supports Dell's U.S. Consumer and Small Business sales segments, along with the global customer contact centers that support those segments, and I support Dell's global privacy compliance function. I have found that the work is more challenging in-house, and I thoroughly enjoy being part of a management team. My time in-house has been much more professionally and personally rewarding than my experience at law firms.

Carolyn: My path to an in-house position was much different than Janet's, although my reasoning was much the same. Before law school, I worked in international development at The World

Bank. Having studied French, I used my language skills in a francophone African division. I loved it, but knew that I wanted to get a professional degree. Even after deciding to go to law school, I was more interested in the international studies options than the actual practice of law. As such, I found ways to study and to work overseas during law school. After graduating, I again worked in international development, but this time, from a legal perspective and in a nonprofit organization. I moved into my first in-house position directly from the nonprofit, which was perhaps a more unusual step at the time than it is today.

I joined AXENT Technologies, Inc. as the third lawyer and as a generalist, doing just about everything that a corporate attorney does in an international, publicly traded company. As the company grew, so did my responsibilities, until I was finally acting as General Counsel when the company was acquired by Symantec Corporation in December 2000. My career has been unusual in that I have not moved companies, beyond the event of acquisition.

My roles have changed significantly, however. I have been responsible for intellectual property portfolios and asset management, for any and all revenue-type transactions, for human resources and employment matters, for M&A, corporate, procurement, and real estate. The initial generalist approach has prepared me well for my current business unit specialization, as I am able to spot issues in a general counsel capacity, and to enable more effective results by relying on the various specialists in our organization. As the company has grown, along with our in-house staff with various areas of expertise, my role as a leader has changed and I rely on inside (including my own staff) and outside counsel differently.

Today, I manage a team of nine people, supporting Symantec's Global Services and Support (GSS) organization. I directly support the Group President, leading the GSS organization, as well as all of the global lines of business within the group, including Technical Support, Professional Services (Consulting, Managed Services, and Software as a Service), Education, and specialized areas relating to these services for security response and management. It's a growing and evolving business, which keeps it interesting.

C. Some Thoughts to Consider on Your Path to In-House

Our paths are a good demonstration that there is no one way to establish an international in-house legal career. Where Carolyn began a career in international development, with an interest in several specialties but no primary legal focus, Janet had developed a very specific skill set as a tax attorney. Carolyn worked in international organizations and nonprofits before going in-house to a technology company, where Janet established her expertise in a law firm. Certainly, the path from law firm to in-house is the more traditional route, but many factors can help you and an employer decide if you make the right fit.

So, what can you do now to start preparing? Before law school, a focus on languages, international studies, or a degree with an international interest is a good start. Depending on your career focus, a language skill may be a driving factor. Although French, German, and Spanish are the most widely spoken languages, in today's market, knowing Arabic, Mandarin, or Japanese may create unique opportunities. You may also consider where you want to study. Exchange programs from U.S. universities are great opportunities to immerse yourself in a different culture and to practice language skills. In her third year, Carolyn arranged to do an exchange with a student at the University of Paris law school. It was a challenge, but it posed unique opportunities as well. Being fully immersed into the French law school, she learned about not only the French legal system, but also the process of learning, impressions of French and other foreign law students, and how to take oral exams in French. It was daunting, at times, but a rewarding experience overall.

If you are considering law school outside the United States, you will find advantages and disadvantages. Many schools outside of the United States are less expensive, but you will likely want to consider obtaining an LLM from a well-known U.S. university afterward. You may also consider the reverse scenario, obtaining a J.D. from a U.S. school and doing some post-J.D. studies at a foreign school. Bar reciprocity is something that you should consider, whether you want to practice in or outside the United States or in several countries. Depending on where you work and what you do, the definition of practicing law may vary, and representation may not require local qualification. This is particularly true of in-house work.

If you are practicing now, remember that the very best in-house lawyers working on international legal topics all started out as good lawyers. Whether they have an expertise that they apply globally or an international background that they apply to legal work, they are all fundamentally very good lawyers who spent time finding a job where they could sell those great skills in exchange for the opportunity to work in a global role.

D. Plan or Chance?

Just as you can take numerous paths to forge your career in international in-house practice, you must also have a reasonable amount of flexibility in order to seize opportunities as they are presented to you. A well-planned career may not always allow you to keep your eyes and mind open to new opportunities, just as lack of planning and focus may not bring you to a point where opportunities are presented at all.

Carolyn: Prior to law school, I held a second job as a self-employed career hunter (volunteer or pay). I spent countless hours researching international careers and weighing my options. At the current point in my career, I can safely say that my professional development has been a healthy combination of planning, sustained interest, and being in the right place at the right time. It's not about relying on chance, but being a reliable, interested, and engaged person so that opportunities come your way first. An in-house career is not about ego.

To get the best projects, you also have to be willing to take the less-glamorous assignments and to use your time wisely. There is a common notion that in-house work is a 9-to-5 proposition, in contrast to the long hours required at the larger law firms. While in-house counsel is rarely presented with a weekend-consuming project at 5 p.m. on a Friday afternoon, you should not expect to succeed by clock-watching.

I know very few in-house managers who proceeded in their careers by working a 40-hour week. Despite those extra hours, you won't have the luxury of time to spend hours researching the most thorough and safest answer; most often, you have to make a quick judgment call based on the best available information at the time. This willingness to participate in the analysis and assumption of risk is the key to being seen as a business person's lawyer.

In addition to hard work, focus, and flexibility, it's also extremely important to understand how you best fit into a global working environment. Being comfortable among your legal and business colleagues and being able to enjoy your work are also key factors in your career path decisions. In my case, my longevity has been a result of fairly regular evaluation of the environment and my place in it.

In a constantly changing environment, there are both opportunities and challenges. I haven't always felt in sync with the changes of the moment, and it has, at times, taken great efforts and a proactive approach to overcome hurdles and to steer my career in a way that was both rewarding and comfortable.

Janet: The key here is to know yourself. If you like change, seek it out. If you like being the expert, make yourself that. The first means that happenstance will rule, whereas the second means that you need a carefully defined plan.

My career has been more happenstance than plan. I began my career as a tax lawyer—an area that breeds specialists. I thought that I would stay in that area of law and never stray. But one thing I discovered about myself is that I really like change and the challenge of the unknown. If you are that way too, stay open to unexpected possibilities and be prepared to take on an area of the law you have never encountered. My current manager offered me a job as the lead lawyer for a sales segment before she knew which segment would be open. I didn't hesitate for long before I took the role, even though I did not know exactly what the job would be and had no experience in supporting a sales segment.

Another thing you should consider is the type of legal department you are joining. If you are one of three or four lawyers, be prepared to spend one day doing litigation, one day working on the company proxy statement, and the next day negotiating a software license. If you like variety and the challenge of something new, you will enjoy a smaller department. Larger departments have generalist jobs too, but they also tend to house specialists who spend all of their time solely in their area of expertise. If you are a specialist and want to stay that way, look at larger departments.

E. Thoughts on Finding the Right Fit for You

While the following considerations are certainly not exhaustive of all that you might consider in making the decision to join a global company's legal department, they are at least a starting point from which you may ask additional questions.

If you are considering going in-house, do your research well. Consider whether size, industry, location of headquarters, and current international practice are important to you. We all have different priorities, and you should follow your interests in selecting the right environment for you. Consider your end goals and where you will have the most enjoyable experience. The work in a $100-million company is not less interesting or less complex than in a $100-billion company. If you are interested in being the General Counsel at a younger age, a smaller company will offer you that opportunity sooner.

Janet: Once you identify a company in which you are interested, and that is interested in you, find out everything you can about the company, its business, and the relevant industry. If you have the ability, get some information from lawyers who have worked in, for, or with the legal department as well. If you don't have those contacts, you need to get as much information as you can when you interview. Questions you should ask include:

- What is the structure of the legal department, and where does the department fit into the company structure? Does the General Counsel report to the CEO?

- How is the department viewed by others in the business? Does Legal have a seat at the table with the business team, or is it viewed as an adversary?

- What is the relationship between the department and the Board? Does the General Counsel attend Board meetings?

- What are the expectations for the role you are considering? How will you know in one year whether you have been successful?

- How do members of the Legal team view their clients? Do they talk about them as colleagues and partners or as adversaries?

- How do the lawyers in the department view each other? Are there legal teams for different divisions, and do they work together or do they compete?

- If you are a specialist, how high up is the most senior specialist in your area? Does she report to the General Counsel? Is she the General Counsel? Or is she five levels down from the General Counsel? Wherever she is, is that a job to which you would aspire?

- Does the Legal department encourage developing relationships with colleagues at other companies?

- How does the department focus on professional development? Are outside learning opportunities encouraged? Do lawyers rotate though various roles in the department? Are mentors common or rare?

Carolyn: I recommend to anyone looking at a change to move in-house or in seeking opportunities that will expand international exposure, to truly explore the environment, including current job descriptions. Are careers built on a generalist approach that is regionally focused or specialist positions that are globally applied? I have a great sense of accomplishment and contribution in my role, but I have had to work extremely hard and diplomatically to gain access.

Where you are in your career may play a big part in your selection of the right department for your current needs, which may include getting some management experience, working overseas for two years, or finding a nest to hopefully make home until retirement. If you are looking for a flexible schedule or a particular salary or a particular location, these may all be factors. For me, having fun and working with people that I respect and enjoy is equally important.

As a woman, the fact that the company I work for is willing to discuss the work-family balance is important to me. I work extremely hard, but I also have many life interests and think that people can lose creativity and perspective if there is no avenue or time to focus on things other than work.

F.   Building International Legal and Business Partner Relationships

Once you find the right job, in order to succeed in a multinational environment, you must be accessible and globally aware. The purpose of global business is to create access and opportunity, and this theme should carry through to your approach as in-house counsel.

Carolyn: By creating access and opportunity, there is a greater give and take, rather than a sense that your gain is at the expense of others. Particularly in a U.S.-based company, there can be great sensitivity to the roles at headquarters as compared to the roles in other regions. A successful international career requires an ability to understand and adjust to different work and cultural environments. If you are viewed as applying your country's ideals and expectations to foreign settings, you will not fit in and you will not be given the access that you desire. This sensitivity should extend to in-country or in-region variations.

Colleagues in international regions may be working alone (i.e., one lawyer in Australia, one in Singapore), whereas we in the United States often have the benefit of a larger team. These international lawyers may feel disconnected from the goals of the department and may have closer relationships with their business colleagues in the region. In some cases, it can be difficult to get the information that you need on a global basis to truly be effective. Here is where prioritization and global awareness are key elements to your success.

You will have to focus your priorities on the greatest needs of your business and rely on regional and specialist resources to help you. You must recognize and appreciate that your regional counsels have the responsibility to support the needs of all the business in their respective territories and that they do not have endless resources to answer every question you might have on how a particular area of law is handled in Australia, Spain, or Saudi Arabia. By helping your regional partners understand the needs of your business and finding ways to make their jobs easier, you will forge better relationships and derive greater value from those relationships over time.

I have found that by creating more efficient ways to share information (i.e., through online resources, training, and playbooks), I help my colleagues save time, provide better answers, and provide more targeted and valuable input to me.

Janet: If you work for a company with locations around the globe, your ability to build e-mail and telephone relationships with colleagues with whom you do not share a common first language or a culture will be the key to your success. You must have exceptionally good relationship skills that can work remotely, and you must be sensitive to other cultures and ways of doing business.

Here are a few steps for connecting with these people: First, find out who you need to know—ask your manager for names of colleagues and clients you need to meet. Second, set up a call with those people and tell them who you are and what you do and ask them about their area of responsibility. Third, take any opportunity you can to meet these people face to face. Travel to see them, and make sure that when they are in your office, you have time to meet with them. Finally, always keep your commitments; if you don't become the person your international colleagues and clients can rely on, you will not be able to succeed in a multinational company.

Two things in particular have worked for me in developing working relationships with my colleagues and understanding the many laws that impact any given project. First, I regularly spend time on the phone with my international colleagues without a specific agenda—we talk about work, projects that are underway, trends we see in the business, our families. That kind of contact helps us get ahead of issues. Second, we have subject-matter calls at Dell: we have a monthly call for all the lawyers involved in privacy compliance, another for all lawyers who support manufacturing facilities, for all lawyers doing employment work, and so on. It's a great way to share information, learn something, and build a sense that we are a global team.

G. Challenges in Networking Outside of Your Company

One of the bigger disappointments to career law firm lawyers who move in-house is the lack of funding and interest in sending counsel to meetings and networking opportunities. It's simply not a priority for in-house counsel to spend time networking outside of the company, and there is not the same level of funding to attend such events. This doesn't mean, however, that we should ignore the importance of networking.

Networking while in-house has to be a priority. When you no longer have to develop business, it's easy to neglect your network. But your network is how you will find people at other companies who can help you with answering legal questions, navigating in-house politics, keeping current on your industry, and perhaps finding your next job. Your biggest challenge will be making yourself get up from your desk and take the time to network.

Start by using the networks that are easily available to you. Join the ABA and participate in relevant sections. If you work for a multinational, we recommend the Section of International Law, because you will find lawyers doing many different types of work around the globe. A local Association of Corporate Counsel chapter is also a good resource, as is your local bar or local networking groups. Don't forget that your company is a corporate citizen—you will also be able to take advantage of networking with businesspeople in your community via volunteerism, chambers of commerce, and community service.

H.   Things to Consider in Business Unit Management

Carolyn: I've seen many newer lawyers come to work in-house and become overly concerned with title and stature or with the ever-elusive glorifying project. Merely finding a job in-house will not make you an insider, and being a trusted business partner is not contingent upon title position or how much experience you have, either external or internal to the company.

Just as with any relationship, you have to develop a level of trust and earn the confidence of your colleagues, both within the legal department and within the business units that you support. Unfortunately, people come to the job with their own biases and expectations, and we often have to prove ourselves repeatedly. Find ways to be invited to meetings by showing interest in the subject matter and offering your thoughts, whether they are legal in nature or business-oriented.

Remember that being a good in-house lawyer requires your understanding of the business goals. To add the best value, I firmly believe that corporate counsel should be an integral part of the business team, at all levels. A true go-to lawyer understands the business needs and the legal requirements to support those needs. The company's executives have to be able to rely on us to enable the business within responsible legal parameters. We must guide the process and create confidence in our leaders.

You will encounter executives who just want to hear "yes" and for you to provide the proverbial rubber stamp. This is not the kind of value-added service that I would advocate, and it certainly does not enable you to gain respect and confidence. Sometimes, I need to say "no" as an absolute, but most of the time, I try to find a way to achieve objectives responsibly. When I do need to draw a more stringent line, I make sure to do this by first expressing my understanding of the situation and then by explaining why certain objectives are not attainable. Being a good business lawyer and demonstrating excellent judgment also means applying the right level of risk to your decisions.

At the same time, a purely business focus could lead you to a point where you are not thinking as a lawyer. It's equally important to keep up with the law and the practice of law in-house. Not only does a good corporate counsel need to understand the law, but he or she must also foresee the trends in how to communicate and interpret the practice of that law. This is often the hardest skill to teach. Each company has its own risk personality, which often changes over time. The Legal department is a key to the pulse of any company's risk profile. Being a part of the business team and balancing risk means that we can't play it 100 percent safe all of the time, but we should demonstrate an ability to take risks with our business partners.

Developing your own personal style is important, because it will allow you to be yourself and feel comfortable in doing what is necessary to get the job done. It's taken me years to develop and understand my own personal style. I've been accused both of being a tough woman and of being too nice. I think it's often harder for women to become comfortable with their business style: What is the appropriate level of push back? How confident should we behave? My personal belief is that you should be true to your own personality. I don't try to be someone different at work than I am in my personal life, with the exception of a level of professionalism and appropriate formality.

Janet: For an in-house lawyer, "just say no" is not the motto. A successful in-house lawyer is part of a business management team that consists of a CEO or division manager, a finance manager, a controller, a sales leader or other business expert, a lawyer, and so on. As part of that team, the lawyer must understand the company's plans and goals, its industry landscape, its customer needs, and its appetite for risk, and must work as part of a team executing a plan in the most profitable, most cost-advantaged, least risky, and absolutely legally compliant manner. Most of the lawyer's time is not spent deciding whether a course of action is legal—instead, the focus is risk assessment.

You must be able to quickly evaluate how much risk flows from the actions that implement the strategic plan, whether that risk can be decreased without detracting from the business goal, and whether the remaining inherent risk is worth achieving the goal. There are also times when the lawyer must play the police officer as well, ensuring that the activities of the company comply with the law or do not take on inappropriate risk.

If you are beginning to envision a tightrope walk, you are getting the picture. You must have good business judgment and be able to work as part of a management team, but you must also be able to think independently and when necessary either find another, less risky way to accomplish the team's goal, or in some cases, be willing to say no, while trying to maintain your status as a respected business partner and avoid becoming the dreaded sales prevention team.

I. Managing Other Lawyers

Good lawyers can make great managers, but poor management rarely leads to a talented and successful staff. Finding a strong manager and being part of a talented management team can make all the difference to your in-house experience.

Carolyn: In-house departments tend not to have the structure in place where career development and morale are big topics of discussion. It can often be taken for granted that lawyers are so grateful to move in-house from the stereotypical work farm attitude in a law firm that management forgets about key factors for development and retention of staff. It's easy to forget that an engaged, happy, and motivated workforce does a better job and makes the jobs of others easier.

I have found that there is ample opportunity in an in-house environment to influence how management should focus on its employees. I have also realized that no role that I have held has ever been as important as my role as a manager. The energy that I put in to ensure that my staff feels valued and that they have opportunity to grow has been far more than any efforts I have made to indulge in an individual project. I spend extra time to create programs to train staff and to develop standards for development. I also make sure that we have time to team-build in new and fun ways—sometimes, this may be a skills-related activity, and sometimes it may be pure fun.

Where there have been conflicts among team members, I have stepped in to help resolve differences and grow relationships. I not only need my staff to trust me, but also to trust and rely on their colleagues so that I am not a one-stop shop for information and approvals. By relying more on each other, we are also a more creative team.

It is also important to recognize and reward other leaders on the team and to create opportunities for individuals to shine. Over time, I have learned to recognize the strengths and weaknesses of my staff so that I can help them excel where they are strongest, and to develop where they have room to grow. It's not only important to manage your staff, but also to lead outward and upward. Think beyond the parameters of the Legal department; reach out to legal colleagues in other regions and other groups.

Good management includes some of the networking that was discussed earlier. I also learned recently that good management means letting go. I recently took an extended vacation—after much planning and preparing, I succumbed to the humble reality that the company could go on without me and, by doing so, created an opportunity for other team members to step up to new experiences. Rather than being fearful that I have proven myself unnecessary, I believe that I will come back to a stronger and more capable team and, with this strength, I also believe that I will have new opportunities for growth. I also found it interesting that, rather than creating an impression that I am no longer committed, I have been complimented by my colleagues for being a strong manager and leader in creating opportunities for others.

Janet: It's fairly rare in a law firm to have a manager, but you do have a lot of bosses. Partners who give you work, your department head, your mentors, and your clients. In-house you will have a manager and you may also become a manager, both of which require skills that law firms will not teach you. But if you want to succeed in-house, you have to become a good manager who can build a solid team.

I have a lot of responsibilities to my team. It's my job to assist each of them with the legal issues they are working on, help them develop into better lawyers, make sure they are not working too hard but also have enough work, keep them on track with their projects, ensure that performance and development plans are in place and that we take the time to act on them, challenge them to be both independent thinkers and good business partners, and act as a navigator through the myriad politics of the corporation.

Building and managing a great team can be one of the most satisfying parts of an in-house career, but you should not approach it as an easy task for which you are well-prepared. Watch the good managers in your organization, study their habits, work for them if you can, and ask one of them to mentor you.

J.   Selecting and Managing Outside Counsel

The basics always ring true—find a counsel that is responsive, understands your business, doesn't try to go around you, and offers sage, business-friendly, current, and accurate advice.

Janet: Outside counsel can be your greatest asset, but they can also be a huge headache. Select the right outside counsel for what you need done, make sure they understand that you are the client and you are in control, and then manage them closely.

There are a variety of reasons you might be looking for outside counsel. Often you simply need local counsel in a country in which you do not have a lawyer. Or you might be looking for specific expertise. You might be under-resourced and need to send out your overflow. Avoid hiring your friends and relatives. Hire to fit the need, whether that is a well-known global expert in the field or just a solid business lawyer from around the corner to get a contract done. Find out what your company's policies are. Do you have the authority to hire outside counsel? Do you get to pick, or must you hire from an approved list? Are there particular outside counsel who have already earned the respect and trust of your new colleagues?

Once you find the right lawyer for your needs, negotiate costs and set expectations. You need to plan your budget, so you need to know what a project will cost. Your outside counsel needs to understand the business, your goal for the project, and most especially that you are the client. There are few things worse than an outside counsel that goes around you and gives an answer directly to your internal client without understanding the business ramifications of the answer.

Carolyn: In addition to the criteria already discussed, in a multinational company, you must also consider the international savvy of your individual counsel or the firm and the consistency of their advice. Just because you are comfortable with the counsel you use in San Diego, doesn't mean that their colleague in London has the same style and reliability. Look at where your business is growing and consider in advance what regional needs you may have, including interpretation of law and translation services. Prepare for your resourcing needs and anticipate costs—outside counsel is a big part of the annual budgeting considerations for a legal department.

It's important to set expectations and to understand your company's direction with respect to legal costs: Is the company prepared to invest in more permanent in-house counsel (and it is your job to advise them if you think it's appropriate), or are the current issues temporary and best allocated to outside counsel? Overflow costs should be budgeted and planned for—otherwise, you risk either giving up your life by working nights and weekends, or giving up your reputation by not being able to manage your work effectively. The reserves for legal costs associated with big-ticket items such as litigation and M&A are all part of the General Counsel's planning process. In some companies, these costs are not part of the legal budget, but are allocated to specific cost centers.

In managing outside counsel, it's important to be clear in your communications by stating not only what you want, but also what you *don't* want. Outside counsel will try to be thorough and will usually set expectations on time and cost, but it is your responsibility to manage this process. Depending on your regular needs, you may choose one counsel upon whom you rely exclusively. In other areas, you may decide that a little competition is the best way to keep costs down and information current. You should also consider what other factors are important to you and your company beyond cost and reliability (and discuss with your management as needed), such as global offices or affiliations, diversity, and even personality (is the firm too formal for your company?).

Along with cost, I'll freely admit that I welcome a free gift with purchase. I appreciate an outside counsel that anticipates my needs, not just by shopping opportunities to their colleagues (e.g., "I see that you've been sued for trademark infringement in Lithuania, and I'd like to introduce you to my colleague."), but also by anticipating my needs in the business context (e.g., providing me with a template form or a summary of a new law). A counsel who is in tune with your company and its competitors and who is interested in helping you provide superior legal service is going to preserve a longer-term relationship.

K. Specialization: Benefit or Barrier to Promotion?

There are many different theories on the best way to gain access to the most-coveted in-house positions or to develop a career that will lead you to a General Counsel position. By now, you should recognize our theory that many paths can lead you to your goal. The question of whether to specialize and, from there, in which topics to specialize is an individual choice, and your ability to move in different directions is not always dependent on your specialization.

Carolyn: I developed my career more as a generalist, and it has suited me well so far, but there are many times when I thought that a specialization would have benefited my career. Because of my interest in an international practice, certain topics lend well to a multinational business setting, including corporate law, tax, intellectual property, or litigation (particularly if you have experience managing cross-regional disputes). Depending on your particular strategy, your career development choices may vary.

If, for instance, you want to go in-house and you currently specialize in employment law, then you might want to seek opportunities to diversify your experiences. If you think that you eventually want to move out of law and into a business role, this may also impact your decisions. I know an employment law specialist who moved from an in-house legal position to the head of human resources, and I know a tax lawyer who is now responsible for international M&A.

There are endless examples of exceptions to the rules, and your choices should follow your goals. If you have a specialty that you are committed to and one for which there is an ongoing need, there is no reason why you shouldn't enjoy a healthy career in that area. If, however, you want to manage a staff with broader responsibilities, then it will be important to find opportunities to expand your experience. The opposite is also true: if you have built a career on good legal sense applied to a variety of situations, you will rely on outside counsel in a different way for more specialized tasks, and if you want to be a General Counsel, then you should consider deepening your experience in specialized areas such as management of litigation, asset management (including intellectual property), corporate law, and M&A.

Janet: Specialization is not a barrier to promotion, but it can become a barrier to becoming General Counsel. That is not always true, but if you are a specialist and you want to stay that way, it's generally a good idea to look for a larger company with a larger department. Find out how high the specialists in that department go. Is the General Counsel a specialist? Are her direct reports specialists? Can a specialist become a Vice President, or is the lead trademark or real estate or ERISA lawyer, for example, a senior counsel? Make sure that the specialists in that company have levels of responsibility and are working on projects that fit with your career goals.

L.   A Few Things You Should Know if You Want to Be General Counsel

We'll start with the reality check again: there is the General Counsel that graduated from law school last year and is helping his buddy with a start-up venture, and then there is the General Counsel who seemingly speaks as though she has taken presentation skills training from Charleton Heston—if she says it, it must be true. Naturally, the challenges and considerations are vastly different for management of a small, privately held company than those of a large publicly traded company, and we cannot hope to cover them all.

Janet: The most respected General Counsels are usually exceptional people. They have great leadership abilities and outstanding business judgment, communicate very well, have executive presence, tend to be very calm even in the face of calamity, and have an uncanny knack for convincing people that spending time and money on compliance and governance is of utmost importance. They don't wait for problems to appear—they learn the business, anticipate the problems, and then avoid them. Like chess masters, it is second nature for them to quickly analyze the business ramifications of a legal decision. They also tend to be people who are in the right place at the right time, either by luck or exceptionally careful planning.

If you want to be a General Counsel, you should get as much experience as you can by practice, practice, practice. Find a great mentor and try to work for a great General Counsel. Focus on developing all the skills you will need, including outstanding business judgment and strategic agility.

Carolyn: In many ways, the General Counsel is the ultimate go-to lawyer and the ultimate leader. The General Counsel needs to understand the business at the highest levels and needs to develop and lead staff who can enable the prioritization of legal requirements and needs, the growth and support of company priorities, and a vision for the department, as it fits within the company. General Counsels can be seen as visionaries and the ultimate judge to determine the values, level of risk assumption, and even the personality and influence of the Legal department. First and foremost, the General Counsel sees the company as the client.

Where the various counsel and subgroups may have competing priorities, the General Counsel must decide how to allocate resources and support the business. In a publicly traded company, the General Counsel will usually be the authority to present to the board of directors and to be accountable to the public and governmental authorities on matters of compliance. The General Counsel is not only an advocate for the company, but is also the voice representing its ethical obligations. In the post–Sarbanes-Oxley world, in the wake of scandal and subsequent regulation, the General Counsel has an even bigger and more important role to balance the ethical, purely legal, and business advisory responsibilities.

My advice is that if you want to be a General Counsel, follow many of the principles outlined in this chapter: understand your business, manage a responsible and insightful budget, create key relationships both internally and externally, keep current with the law, be a go-to lawyer, master your role as risk manager, have a vision, achieve balance, and lead an exceptional staff with reliable and talented outside counsel.

M. Conclusion

Many roads can lead to a successful career as in-house counsel for a multinational company. The path you follow will be unique, and we hope that the advice in this chapter will help you make key choices along the way. Certainly, many factors will influence your direction. The key is not in knowing exactly what you require every step of the way, but in focusing on smaller goals and, if you know your ultimate goal, setting a flexible strategy to help you make important decisions.

You may find, as we have, that your direction and goals may change as you gain exposure to new areas. Hopefully, you will find the road less traveled to be an adventure well worth pursuing and the opportunities vast and exciting.

Fair Winds and Following Seas: A Career in Admiralty Practice

8

by Michael Marks Cohen

A. Introduction

Admiralty is the granddaddy of all international commercial law, with antecedents that stretch back to Biblical times. For more than 500 years, there have been written maritime codes covering carriage of goods by sea, general average, salvage, marine insurance, seamen's rights, and arbitration. In the absence of statutes, judge-made rules have been applied to collision, shipboard personal injury, carriage of passengers, shipbuilding, ship finance, and ship chartering. In modern times, these traditional subjects have been supplemented by shipping regulation and water pollution. Although now there are many treaties and much local legislation, the courts continue to play a very active role in shaping the law to changing circumstances.

Like 60 to 70 percent of my generation, I was drawn to the admiralty bar by seagoing experiences, having served for three years as a naval officer on a destroyer between college and law school at Columbia. At the time, many individuals opted for naval or Coast Guard service rather than be drafted into the Army during the period between the Korean and Vietnam wars. One consideration was to parlay our legal training and military experience into a career, so we could put our time in the service to good use. After clerking for Stanley H. Fuld, the chief judge of the New York Court of Appeals, I started out in maritime practice as a trial lawyer with the Admiralty & Shipping Section of the U.S. Department of Justice in Washington, D.C. Three years later, I joined an admiralty law firm in Manhattan, and I have been in private practice there ever since. Currently I am of counsel to Nicoletti Hornig and Sweeney.

Admiralty principles and concepts are generally similar throughout the world. In many respects, maritime law is a sort of written and unwritten uniform commercial code that has been adopted by each country with local variations. Foreign precedents—especially those from England and other common law jurisdictions like Canada, Australia, New Zealand, Hong Kong, Singapore, and South Africa—are frequently cited and are regarded as very persuasive. There is a good deal of maritime litigation in the United States, mostly in the federal courts, since federal law is controlling. Generally, apart from personal injury cases, there are no jury trials.

Maritime law strives for uniformity. New developments are, therefore, followed not just locally but nationally and internationally. Moreover, it is the only area of federal law where older cases are commonly more highly regarded than more recent ones, partly because maritime matters formed such a substantial part of the work of the Supreme Court up until just after World War I. A remarkable number of current procedures in federal civil litigation, which are intended to promote fairness and simplicity, have their origin in admiralty practice—some of it more than 150 years old and/or of foreign derivation. Routinely, many disputes are not taken to court at all but instead are voluntarily submitted to arbitration in London or New York, often before commercial arbitrators rather than lawyers.

B. Disadvantages

There are a few disadvantages in admiralty practice. Most cases involve claims of less than $250,000; few go as high as $10 million. Such blockbusters as the *Titanic, Andrea Doria, Amoco Cadiz,* and *Exxon Valdez* come along only once every decade or so. Hardly ever is there a case that will make or break the client. Although world events have an immediate impact on the day-to-day practice, in reality, shipping involves the legs rather than the heart of world trade.

Compensation is adequate but not fabulous. Much of the work comes from a comparatively small number of marine insurance companies, a situation that fosters price competition. In addition, the nature of the work makes it difficult to leverage— that is, to put more than one associate on a case with a partner. These factors force admiralty lawyer income levels below those of colleagues in other fields.

Shipping is not an explosively expanding field. Moreover, it is susceptible to large cyclical swings. Very few new domestic shipping companies are formed. Established companies do not change legal advisers very often. Most new clients are referrals from existing clients, or from local corporate law firms, or from out-of-state or foreign admiralty lawyers.

C. Advantages

For all of the disadvantages cited, there are quite a number of advantages to the practice. Because of the historical role of London in marine insurance, salvage, ship finance, and ship chartering, all admiralty lawyers and their clients throughout the world speak English. It is not necessary to be fluent in a foreign language to have a successful practice and a rewarding career.

The bar is small—almost a craft guild—with only a few thousand full-time practitioners here and abroad. Frequent contacts among the lawyers are maintained across state lines and international boundaries. Locally, in the cities where they practice, admiralty lawyers have a well-deserved reputation for professionalism and courtesy in their relations with one another. There are several unusually active national and international bar associations. The number of maritime lawyers practicing together in a firm is usually small. In New York, many of the maritime firms concentrate on shipping law, with perhaps some additional work in aviation and the sale of bulk commodities that are shipped by sea, such as oil, grain, and sugar. A few New York firms, and one or two others elsewhere in the country, may have as many as two dozen admiralty partners and associates, but for the most part, there are usually fewer than 10 maritime lawyers in any given firm. Increasingly, those lawyers can be found as a small department of a large corporate law firm.

There are frequent opportunities for travel to interesting places—most often London, Tokyo, and Hong Kong. Clients tend to be very practical, often colorful figures. The risks in shipping appeal to individuals who enjoy gambling for high gains in a short period. The sums can be large. Time differences, geographic separation, weather uncertainties, human errors, and the need for quick decisions call for analytical skills and imaginative tactics that are not usually found in a nonmaritime commercial practice. It is definitely not a stuffy field.

Practice is very closely tied to the headlines in the newspapers. Natural disasters such as earthquakes and hurricanes, as well as predictable seasonal events, such as ice in the Great Lakes, promptly cause clients to seek advice. The same is true for world events—war in the Persian Gulf, pirates off Singapore, refugees fleeing in small boats at sea, the decline of the dollar, turmoil in South America. When combined with individual calamities—groundings, oil pollution, boiler breakdown, pilfered liquor, rotting fruit, leaking holds—the work can be very stimulating. It is not only intellectually challenging but fast-moving: lawyers are commonly called for spot advice while a crisis is in progress.

The overall lifestyle in maritime practice is generally much more relaxed than for large corporate work. Time can usually be found for bar association efforts, teaching, writing for professional journals, and, most important of all, being with family. Practicing admiralty law ought not to destroy your marriage or ruin your children. In recent years, a very high percentage of associates joining admiralty firms have been women. There is widespread religious diversity at the bar. Greater racial diversity would be welcome.

D. Training

Although not essential, an admiralty course in law school would be helpful, not only for careers in practice but also for those seeking clerkships with federal judges in port cities. Experience at sea with the Navy, Coast Guard, or Merchant Marine is useful but, again, not a prerequisite. Perhaps the best training for admiralty practice is to write an article on a maritime law subject for a student journal in law school.

E. Starting Out

A good place to start out is the Torts Branch of the U.S. Department of Justice. Nearly all admiralty cases involving the federal government are handled centrally by about a dozen admiralty lawyers in Washington, D.C. and San Francisco. There are a few openings annually.

In private practice, New York is by far the biggest market. There are new jobs for perhaps two dozen associates with maritime firms there each year. Outside New York, all of the major seaports, the Great Lakes, and the inland rivers combined may produce an equal number of openings. Firms can be difficult to locate just through Martindale-Hubbell, but many of the leading firms are identified in the *Chambers USA Guide* and *The Best Lawyers in America*. All firms that have at least one lawyer who is a member of the Maritime Law Association of the United States (MLA) are listed at the MLA web site, www.mlaus.org.

The China Bug

9

by Michael E. Burke

A. Introduction

The first thing you should know about me is that I'm very proud to be from New Jersey. When I was growing up, my father told me, almost daily: "What New Jersey makes, the world takes." He was right. New Jersey is a very international place. My hometown is a bedroom community for New York City and Northern New Jersey business markets, meaning that many people from my hometown traveled around the world. The local companies, such as AT&T and Schering-Plough, were always doing something outside the United States or bringing non-U.S. employees to New Jersey. On my block, we had first-generation immigrant families from Ireland, India, and other places. There were also many second-generation immigrant families. New York City, perhaps the most international city in the world, was 25 miles away. Growing up in New Jersey meant, to me, understanding that we were part of a larger, global community. In some ways, I always assumed that business, including the practice of law, was inherently international.

Being from New Jersey also means living by a certain work ethic. My first job, in eighth grade, was working for my uncle's landscaping company. Landscaping in the New Jersey summer heat is a tough job. The worst days were when we had to visit the dump. My uncle was the toughest boss I have ever had; he expected me to be at work every day, work hard each day, and to do things right the first time. Living up to that ethic—taking pride in what you do, and doing your job to the best of your ability every day (even on the days where you'd rather be doing something else)—is an important first step in becoming an international lawyer. In order to be a good international lawyer, you need to be willing to invest the time and effort in building your skills, and you need to provide your best service to your clients every day.

B. Getting Educated

I never had a "Eureka!" moment about becoming a lawyer, and it wasn't one of my childhood dreams. There were plenty of lawyers in my hometown, but I don't remember being inspired by any of them to practice law. My real childhood dream was to occupy right field for the Boston Red Sox, but my lack of athletic ability got in the way. In fact, I always thought that I would be a college history professor. All of this is to suggest that one doesn't need to be specifically inspired to become a lawyer.

Although I didn't really think about becoming a lawyer, I was very interested in international relations and history. I was the kid who always participated in the model United Nations program. I even took a college course at Boston College (during the summer between my junior and senior high school years) on Soviet foreign policy, and then convinced one of my high school history teachers that I should spend part of my senior year doing an independent study project on Soviet history. Further, I was very fortunate that my parents took me—and sometimes sent me—overseas to learn about different countries and cultures. Obviously, the international bug bit me before the lawyer bug.

I attended the University of Michigan for my freshman year of college, and that's where the international bug began to change into a China bug, although the China bug took a long time to develop. Kenneth Lieberthal was the professor in the Comparative Politics class I took during my freshman year. That class was taught at the same time Professor Lieberthal was writing his seminal work *Governing China: From Revolution Through Reform*, and he brought a lot of his research and observations about China into the classroom. That class was the first time I remember thinking that China was a place about which I wanted to learn much more.

After my freshman year, I transferred to Georgetown University's School of Foreign Service (SFS). The SFS has perhaps the most challenging, most internationally focused curriculum of any college-level program in the United States. I'm fortunate to have been able to complete that program, and it was the perfect fit for my interest in international affairs. While at SFS, I studied abroad at the Catholic University of Antwerp in Belgium, passed my foreign language proficiency exam in French, and wrote two theses, one on conflict resolution in Northern Ireland and one on defense and security integration within the European Union.

Discussion of my college experience does have relevance for lawyers who wish to practice international law. Good international lawyers know more than one language, and college is one of the best places to become multilingual. Also, good international lawyers appreciate and can operate in other cultures. College is one of the best places to become exposed to other cultures, such as through club activities or study abroad programs. If you didn't learn a foreign language in college or study abroad, there are opportunities to do so after college and even during law school.

After college, I worked for Exxon Research and Engineering in New Jersey, developing cost models and estimates for overseas refinery projects, including a project in China's Tarim Basin. I also worked for U.S. Senator Dianne Feinstein as a staff assistant, opening and responding to constituent letters and requests that touched on foreign affairs issues. After the close 1994 Congressional mid-term election (because of my boss's very close call), I realized that I had to get some sort of advanced degree, and my strong preference was to enter law school.

C.   Law School: What, When, and How?

I know that attendees at the Section of International Law's *Path-ways* programs, which features experienced international lawyers offering guidance to law students and young lawyers on develop-ing an international practice, often have specific questions about how to direct their law school experience so they can practice international law after graduation. I have a few answers, based on my experiences.

Law students sometimes ask whether they should go to, or transfer to, a specific law school in order to become an interna-tional lawyer. My belief is that students should attend the law school where they feel the most comfortable and believe they have the best chance at completing a comprehensive legal educa-tion, and not necessarily worry about whether a certain school has a robust international curriculum. Most law schools now have some form of international law curriculum. There are also interna-tional law summer programs that may supplement your school's existing curriculum.

At *Pathways* programs, I am often asked whether there are any specific classes one should take in law school in order to become an international lawyer. The answer is "maybe." Consider taking an introduction to international law course, if one is offered by your school. You might also consider taking other international law courses if they are of interest to you. But there is no strict blueprint of law school classes that will create an international lawyer, and as stated previously, some of the essential skills for an international lawyer (e.g., language and cross-cultural appre-ciation) may not be offered as part of a law school curriculum.

I graduated Georgetown University Law Center (GULC) in 1998. I was fortunate that GULC has a robust international cur-riculum, but I chose GULC because it was in Washington, was a comfortable place, and offered a great legal education. GULC's international law curriculum was a bonus, but wasn't necessarily one of the primary factors in my decision to attend. Put another way, you should attend the program where you think you have the best chance to excel.

At GULC, I took the introduction to international law course, the international trade and investment course, and courses on

European Union and Korean law, respectively. I also took courses on venture capital transactions, alternative dispute resolution, corporate taxation, and trusts and estates. I served on the staff of, and as an editor for, the journal *The Tax Lawyer*. One should seek a well-rounded legal education—take courses from a wide range of areas, including international law. Don't feel obligated to take every possible international law course, and don't feel that your legal education is lacking if a school offers only a few international law courses. Participate in a journal, even if it does not focus on international law. The point of law school is to produce well-rounded lawyers, who are versed in several areas of the law and who can think, analyze, communicate, and write effectively.

If your school doesn't have a specific course you're looking for, consider an independent study/directed research project. I would be remiss if I did not mention one of my law school professors and the tremendously positive impact he has had on my career. Jim Feinerman is one of the best-known and best-qualified China experts in the United States. He has studied China for almost his entire life, and he brings an incredible passion to the study of legal development in China. He is also one of the best, most generous people you will ever meet. Professor Feinerman was the professor for the Corporations class I took during the first semester of my second year, and he spent a fair amount of time in that class discussing how corporations were regulated in Japan and China. The comparative analysis struck a cord with me, and I began going to see Professor Feinerman during office hours to discuss Chinese business regulation; the China bug that was planted in Professor Lieberthal's class had begun to find an outlet.

During my second year, GULC did not offer a course each semester on Chinese law (it does now), and I asked Professor Feinerman how I could learn more about the development of the Chinese legal system. Results of these discussions were two supervised research/independent study projects during my second and third years of law school that, in turn, resulted in my first two law review articles. I suggest that you should develop a good relationship with your professors, especially international law professors, and learn from their experience. I am still in contact with Professor Feinerman, and he remains a tremendous resource for me as I continue to develop my career. A professor's value to law students is not limited to the classroom. If your school permits it, think about undertaking a directed study/independent research course; if your school's curriculum seems to be missing a course, don't be afraid to develop one.

D.   Getting a First Job: How, Where, and Why?

At *Pathways* events, law students often ask if, in an interview process, they should indicate an interest in a specific practice area, in order to increase their chances of being assigned international work. It's appropriate to express an interest in an area of the law if you're genuinely interested in that area, but don't express an interest in an area just because you think it is a way to get international work. One of my classmates told interviewers that he wanted to do project finance work. He wasn't really interested in that work, but he thought it was a good way to get international work. He was hired into a project finance group at a large D.C. firm, and he did project finance work for projects in Los Angeles, Phoenix, and Milwaukee. He got frustrated at the lack of international work and left that firm after 18 months. One other note: when approaching a potential interview, you should research the firm and the interviewer, so you can understand what the firm does and does not do in terms of international work. An interviewee once told me that she thought my firm's Korea practice was of interest. We don't have a Korea practice, and her statement was a factor in not inviting her back for a second-round interview.

I am also often asked whether a person who is interested in international law should automatically join a large law firm in New York upon graduation. The practice of international law isn't confined to huge law firms or even to firms in New York. Sophisticated and interesting international legal work can be found in many cities. In determining where to go after graduation, you should consider a place where you can develop your career and can get immediate access to interesting and rewarding work. Also, you might want to think about living in a place where you can have a decent quality of life.

After graduation, I joined a large law firm based in Seattle—quite a change for someone born and raised in New Jersey and educated in Washington, D.C. I was not a summer associate at that firm, and I went west to be a part of the dot-com explosion, with the expectation that a lot of interesting, international work would flow from emerging technology companies. I chose to go to Seattle, and not a firm in New York, because I wanted to get as much client service responsibility as quickly as possible, be able to build an expertise, and be at a place where I thought I could spend the majority of my career.

E. Becoming a Good International Lawyer

When I met my mentor partner on my first day at my first job, he told me, "I always thought international law was a waste of time." Nonetheless, I learned much from my mentor partner. He taught me how to closely read a contract and identify potential problem areas. I knew that he expected me to know how an agreement worked, in addition to the words on the page. He showed me how to economize on words and draft a tight contract. I knew that he expected that the maximum amount be communicated in the least number of words. He hated even the hint of sloppiness in drafting. He also taught me the importance of managing expectations and how to communicate effectively with clients within and outside of the firm. I knew that he expected my work product when I promised it. In addition, he showed me how to organize files efficiently and effectively. He was a good mentor, and he taught me how to be a good lawyer, which was a good thing, because in order to be a good *international* lawyer, you need to be a good lawyer first. That's more than a tautology. The skills needed to become a good lawyer, such as being a good communicator, well organized, a good writer, and a good issue spotter, are doubly important for becoming a good international lawyer. It shouldn't matter if you're building those skills doing noninternational work. You need to do all you can as a young lawyer to build basic practice skills—the building blocks for a long career. Take the time to perfect those skills, because it is a worthwhile investment.

I started doing international work by networking with the firm's other lawyers, understanding who had international work, and offering to help with whatever tasks needed attention. In most cases, having a mentor partner does not preclude you from working for other lawyers in your firm. Don't be shy about volunteering to help out with projects that interest you. Also, be persistent, because you may not get on the first project for which you volunteer, but after a while, you'll find yourself in a core group of go-to lawyers.

Sometimes, in order to become a good international lawyer, you may have to take a risk and step outside traditional legal practice. Some of the most interesting international work is performed at government agencies (like the Office of the U.S. Trade Representative and the State Department), nongovernment organizations, think tanks, and academic institutions. Spending time at such places can enhance a career and be very rewarding. Do not be afraid to step out of a law firm in order to get more international experience. Also, do not agonize over that decision; as long as you are building your career, it doesn't really matter where you get your experience.

I spent five years at my first law firm in Seattle and then in its Washington, D.C. offices. At about the four-and-a-half-year mark, it became clear that I would not be able to meet my professional goals there, and I wanted to spend more time in Greater China. Through my work with the China Committee of the ABA International Section of Law, I had gotten to know some of the people involved with the Asian Institute of International Financial Law (AIIFL) at Hong Kong University's (HKU) Faculty of Law. AIIFL offered me a chance to become a Fellow and spend time at HKU. I really did not want to leave my first firm, but I decided that I would have to in order to get more on-the-ground exposure in Greater China. In retrospect, my decision to join AIIFL was absolutely right.

I spent about two years traveling between Washington, D.C. and Hong Kong as an AIIFL Fellow. At AIIFL, among other things, I was able to work on research projects involving China's securities markets, publish China-related law review articles, and teach a few classes. I also participated in the 2003 Sino-U.S. Legal Exchange Program sponsored by the U.S. Department of Commerce and China's Ministry of Commerce. Most importantly, I got to spend a lot of time in China, and that was the best learning experience of all. I enjoyed my time at AIIFL, but I knew that, at some point, I'd have to return to the United States. You should keep building your contacts network, because you never know when you're going to need it.

F.   Networking, Associations, and Branding

As a young lawyer, you should get involved in bar associations and community groups; they offer opportunities to speak, publish, and learn. These groups can also offer exposure to different cultures and business environments, and provide valuable contacts around the world. In addition, these groups provide a way for lawyers to give back to their communities.

One of the best decisions I have ever made was to become active in the ABA Section of International Law. I joined the Section because it was one of the few bar associations with a China-focused committee. My first step in joining the China Committee was contacting the then-Chair, Jim Zimmerman, and asking how I could help with the committee's activities. Jim asked me to work with the Committee's listserve and Web site. Soon after, I was asked to join the China Committee as a Vice Chair, where I continued to manage the Committee's Web site, started a working group on China's electronic commerce regulations, planned programs at Section events, and wrote the committee's year-in-review articles.

I owe a debt to Jim Zimmerman for supporting my efforts to become active in the China Committee. Without his encouragement, I would not have been able to become active in the Section of International Law. I have found that the Section is different from many other bar associations, because most of our leaders are like Jim—we're open and encouraging to young lawyers, and we operate, for the most part, as a meritocracy. The Section enables young lawyers to be as involved as they wish to be, on their own schedule. It has been a wonderful platform on which to build my brand.

As a young lawyer, you should also build your brand by taking on speaking and writing opportunities. One of the best decisions I made as a first-year associate with my first firm was to partner with the Seattle office of the U.S. Department of Commerce on a series of talks about the implications of the European Union's adoption of the Euro. Through these presentations, I was able to meet current and potential clients, demonstrate an expertise, and generate good public relations for my firm. I was also able to publish several law review articles on China-related topics, each of which helped build my brand.

I joined my current firm in 2005, and I was able to identify my next career step and successively join my current firm through the contacts I made through the Section. I am currently the Chair of the firm's China Practice Group, and we're busily building out our capacity to serve our clients on China-related matters.

G. Conclusion

I hope that this overview has been helpful, and I know that some parts may be more relevant than others, based on the particular reader. You should view my experience in such a light, and should feel free to determine whether my guidance should impact your own career development. Put another way, my experience is illustrative, and you should make up your own mind about how to develop your career.

I hope that you take away from this chapter an understanding that an international legal career is what one makes of it; you should take ownership of your destiny and challenge yourself to build the career you want. A final piece of advice and a request: being a lawyer is a serious job, involving long hours, demanding clients, and serious issues, but the job should be fun (or at least parts of it). So, while you should take your job and work product seriously, consider taking yourself a little less seriously.

A Career in International Commercial Arbitration

10

by Marc J. Goldstein

A. Introduction

The proper path in life often is learned by not following it. So it was for me, in my career in international litigation and arbitration. I went to law school determined to become a fire-breathing courtroom lawyer. I never took a specialized class in international dispute resolution, because this seemed a distant and irrelevant body of knowledge. Today, I would urge all aspiring litigators, and even aspiring corporate lawyers, to take that course, because application of the principal international agreements on arbitration will probably be unavoidable in life as a lawyer. A working knowledge of these treaties on the enforcement of arbitration agreements and awards, and how those treaties are enforced in the courts of the United States, is essential working knowledge—part of the litigator's working vocabulary in the same sense as the Federal Rules of Civil Procedure. The same may be said for the arbitration rules of the leading international arbitration institutions (e.g., International Chamber of Commerce [ICC], American Arbitration Association [AAA], London Court of International Arbitration, and various institutional rules based on the United Nations Commission on International Trade Law [UNCITRAL] Rules).

Similarly, after following the linear path from law school to a large New York City law firm, I only discovered through contacts with others undreamt-of career possibilities: clerkships with international tribunals; study programs in comparative law and civil law at foreign law schools; counsel positions with major international arbitral institutions; apprenticeships with foreign law firms; and associate positions in foreign offices of U.S. law firms.

B. From New York to the Hague

My own introduction to international arbitration was involuntary: I was drafted, as a young associate, from a budding career as an antitrust and securities litigator to devote most of my time to a complex expropriation case before the Iran-U.S. Claims Tribunal in The Hague. This was not necessarily considered a plum assignment for an associate in the mid-1980s, a few years before globalization became a hot topic in the legal profession. I spent nearly four years in a state of deep ambivalence. While my peers were taking and defending depositions, and even trying cases before juries in state and federal courts, I was learning the complexities of the valuation of nationalized property in international law, the discounted cash-flow method, principles of accounting for real estate development projects, and more about the construction industry than I would ever have cared to know. But I was also learning important lessons—although I perhaps did not realize it at the time—about cross-cultural communications in the legal profession, evidence in international tribunals, and how jurists from different legal cultures can evaluate the same set of facts in dramatically different ways.

Along the way, I also had personal experiences that my peers did not share: roasted reindeer in Malmo, Sweden; swimming in the North Sea; hearings in the Czar Nicholas room of the Peace Palace in The Hague. And I had my first exposure to the courtesy culture of international arbitration: the numerous shared meals, coffee breaks, and cocktails that surrounded the proceedings and brought lawyers into contact with arbitrators in ways that are unheard of in bench-bar relations in the United States.

My experience at the Iran-U.S. Claims Tribunal also exposed me to an important dimension of international arbitration—its vast literature. This was a field where professors acted as lawyers, lawyers wrote for publication as if they were professors, and the line between academia and practice was blurred in the ranks of arbitrators and counsel. Moreover, this was a field where active practitioners kept up with the literature. Because of the tradition of confidentiality of arbitration proceedings, the scholarly literature in the field assumes a special importance for the exchange of ideas. The lesson for a career-building young practitioner in this field was clear: publication could be a most worthwhile activity, a way to make an impact and contribute to one's reputation in the field in an effective way.

C. Choosing a Law Firm

Good advice to the aspiring lawyer in this field also includes suggestions on the choice of a law firm. In a sense, such advice does not differ very much from what one would say about any specialized field: join a firm with an established practice. But in the field of international dispute resolution, some special considerations may apply. First, join a firm with a large and established practice in international commercial transactions. International arbitrations originate in contracts; parties to contracts often are loyal and continuing clients of the lawyers who drafted the contracts for them. One of my earliest international commercial arbitrations, after my experience in the Iran-U.S. Claims Tribunal, was for a U.S. company that had been a client of my firm for more than three decades. The contract containing the arbitration clause had been signed in 1979; the dispute arose in 1990. The client was loyal and called us immediately.

A second suggestion is to join a firm where you will have the privilege to work as an apprentice to one of the world's leading international arbitrators. International arbitration remains one of the most exclusive professional clubs in the world, and even the new practitioner can identify its members relatively easily.[1] In large international commercial arbitrations, it is usually the privilege of the presiding arbitrator to select an associate to act as law secretary to the Tribunal—the equivalent of a judicial law clerk—who studies the parties' memorials, evaluates the evidence, researches the legal questions, and drafts orders and awards.

Once you have found a place in this specialty, build your career by being a writer and a joiner. Identify the major publications followed by the international arbitration bar around the world, and find time to contribute articles to them.[2] Be a member of the international arbitration or international litigation committee of your local bar association. Join the ABA Section of International Law and Practice, and become active in its International Dispute Resolution Committee. Consider membership in the Institute for Transnational Arbitration, the Corporate Counsel Committee of the American Arbitration Association, and the American Society of International Law. Participate in one of the Fellowship courses offered by the United Kingdom's Chartered Institute of Arbitrators, and become a Fellow by passing the Fellowship examination. Attend the meetings of the organizations you join, and become a friend and colleague of fellow practitioners around the world. Identify the organizations, including the ICC Court of Inter-

---

[1] See, for example, the membership list of the International Council on Commercial Arbitration (ICCA), which can be found in the annual *ICCA Yearbook on Commercial Arbitration*. This is not an exhaustive list, but it is certainly a good start. For a more extensive list of U.S. practitioners, you might subscribe to the newsletters of the Institute for Transnational Arbitration or the ABA Section of International Law and Practice's International Commercial Arbitration Committee.

[2] A short list would include the *Journal of International Arbitration, Arbitration International, American Review of International Arbitration, Mealey's International Arbitration Report*, and the *International Chamber of Commerce Bulletin*.

national Arbitration and the London Court of International Arbitration, that have special committees and special programs for young practitioners.

Further, make your interest and talent in the field known to your colleagues in the firm. Be the first litigator on your floor to master the main legal research sources used by international arbitration practitioners. Once you have learned to navigate the annual *Yearbook of the International Council on Commercial Arbitration* (ICCA), the ICCA Congress Series, the *ICC Bulletin*, and several of the more significant Web sites that track developments in international commercial arbitration (e.g., www.internationaladr.com), you will have made yourself marketable to the more senior practitioners in your firm.

D.   The Rewards of a Career in International Commercial Arbitration

What might be the rewards of a career in the practice of international commercial arbitration? I approach this question with a particular viewpoint, having gradually shifted my practice from one that was predominantly litigation in the state and federal courts to one that is predominantly before international arbitral tribunals.

First, I have found that presenting the case to an arbitral tribunal composed entirely, or substantially, of arbitrators selected by the parties is an intellectually and personally gratifying experience. In some state court systems in the United States, the commercial judges often come to the bench from careers in criminal courts or other civil courts, and infrequently have the experience or enthusiasm for the complex issues that international litigations often present. These are courts of general jurisdiction, crowded with cases of all types, but mainly with cases that involve disputes among local individuals, companies, and governments. The judges often are elected officials, and their level of dedication to legal scholarship will vary widely. The quality of adjudication will generally be better in the federal courts, but if one views the U.S. model of litigation with its emphasis on pretrial discovery as a flawed model, then it is easy to develop an affection for the international arbitration process.

1. Discovery American-Style

This is not the occasion to debate whether discovery American-style does or does not surpass the more hybrid civil law—common law model of evidence-gathering that prevails in international commercial arbitration. This chapter focuses on career selection, and accordingly the young practitioner may wish to consider a reality of the litigation world that is not often mentioned in job interviews. The U.S. adversary system remains a bruising, fractious, confrontational, and frequently discourteous and even vicious process for resolving disputes. Moreover, the discovery process often brings out the worst characteristics of practitioners, as they are largely left without direct judicial supervision to conduct hand-to-hand combat in pretrial exchanges of documents and in depositions. U.S. litigation is not a field for the weak of heart, and many young lawyers who are attracted by the intellectual dimension of litigation ultimately make career decisions against the field precisely because of the inherent unpleasantness of it.

2. Discovery in International Commercial Arbitration

Discovery in international arbitration can be as disorderly and contentious as it is in U.S. litigation, or, more ideally as it is practiced under the guidance of experienced arbitrators, it can be an efficient method to enable each side to determine if the opposing party possesses documents that are material to proving its case. There is frequent occasion for interaction with opposing counsel in well-managed international arbitrations, as counsel will be pressed by the tribunal to reach agreement on procedural matters and provide the tribunal with agreed-on guidelines. Relations are often more collegial than in U.S. litigation, perhaps mainly because the opportunities to pursue delay of the process as a conscious strategy are reduced or eliminated. The result of this process, in my experience, is an elevated level of rhetoric and argument, and less hyperbole, overstatement, misstatement, and ad hominem attacks on opposing counsel. The result is that the most intensely contested matters, even those involving international political animosity and divergent economic positions, can proceed in an environment of utmost courtesy and mutual respect.

3. The Quality of Arbitrators

Further, the arbitral tribunal has been engaged by the parties and/or the arbitral institution specifically to fulfill a mission in this particular case. The arbitrators are not civil servants, nor do they enjoy the lifetime tenure of federal judges in the United States. If a complex case requires extensive written submissions from the parties or an extended number of days or weeks for evidentiary hearings, it is more likely that an international arbitral tribunal, as compared to a domestic court, will devote the time and attention that the matter requires. The arbitrators, for one thing, are compensated for their time. Further, while arbitrators may be busy practitioners with heavy caseloads, their work is conducted under a microscope in ways that the work of domestic judges is not. Because the careers of international arbitrators depend on their reputations, they want to impress one another, the counsel and parties who appear before them, and the arbitral institutions that appointed them—and, particularly in the case of ICC arbitration, have the opportunity to review the arbitrators' awards before they are issued. These factors do not necessarily ensure a better quality of justice than that dispensed in the domestic litigation system, but they do create momentum favoring a high level of scholarship and rigorous analysis in international arbitration awards.

Why should this be a factor of significance in a fledgling lawyer's career selection? The answer is that, unfortunately, economic realities and human frailties limit the quality of justice dispensed by courts. As a litigator in a complex case, you devote tireless effort to the effective presentation of evidence, argument, and authority in support of your client's position. You want to win, but you also want to see your work product treated with the respect it deserves by the decision makers. So does your client, who has paid hundreds of thousands or perhaps millions of dollars for your efforts. You want your arguments, and those of the other side, addressed in a thoughtful and intellectually honest way, in decisions that are carefully and systematically reasoned, and uninfected by the personal bias of the jurist. Because winning and losing cannot be the only measure of your professional satisfaction, you at some point realize that much of your satisfaction is derived from having a jurist or arbitrators who treat the issues and authorities with the same passionate attention that you do. Anyone who reads the international arbitration awards that are published in the *Mealey's International Arbitration Report* cannot help but be struck by the precision with which arbitrators present the contentions of the parties, the care with which they formulate the issues presented for decision, and the comprehensiveness of their analysis and citation of relevant authority.

4. Other Attractions

Other aspects of the international arbitration process may also be attractive to the young lawyer who is interested in dispute resolution practice, but leery of the time demands and stress often said to be associated with litigation practice in large U.S. law firms. First, the limitations on discovery in international arbitration substantially eliminate much of the tedium associated with the production of documents and preparation of responses to interrogatories, tasks that unfortunately but necessarily are assigned to the most junior lawyers on the team in a U.S. litigation. I often cringe at the notion that young lawyers are receiving any training when they are called upon to review hundreds of thousands of documents from a client's files for attorney-client privilege in advance of their production, or to wade through a similar volume of documents produced by an adverse party, or to spend grueling days reviewing the fruits of document discovery from multiple parties and nonparties in a central document repository. There is document discovery in international arbitration, within limitations imposed on a case-by-case basis by the arbitrators, but the influence of civil law systems on the process has made it next to impossible for counsel to successfully request and obtain "all documents referring or relating to" a particular issue or contention. Thus, not only is the production of useless mounds of documents eliminated, but also much of the squabbling among lawyers about whether particular discovery requests are unduly burdensome, and whether the adverse party by objecting is seeking to conceal information that might be germane to the case.

Further, in most international arbitrations, the arbitrators have no effective powers to compel production of documents or other discovery from noncombatants—that is, third parties (except in the rare instance where such parties are domiciled at the place of arbitration, in which case such assistance might be obtained through a local court). This dramatically reduces the scope of potential discovery, as compared to domestic litigation. The result is that international arbitration is rather more directly channeled to the heart of the matter. For the young lawyer, there is the opportunity to be closely involved in shaping the client's litigation strategy, drafting the pleadings, and working with the most significant documentary evidence from your own client's files rather than being preoccupied with the detective work that prevails in U.S. litigation, as adverse parties send teams of young lawyers on the often fruitless quest for the smoking gun in the other party's files.

Another lifestyle issue is the pace of the action. International arbitration is a tightly controlled process in which the arbitral tribunal determines what submissions each party will be permitted to make and when they will be made. The result is that, while work on an international arbitration case certainly can be as intense and time-consuming as any other work in dispute resolution practice, it does tend to follow a relatively stable pattern of "my turn, your turn." The claimant submits its Statement of Claim, and the respondent submits its Answer/Statement of Defense. The claimant submits an application for interim measures of protection, and the respondent submits an opposition to the application. Generally, such submissions are made pursuant to a procedural time table fixed in advance by the arbitral tribunal. This contrasts with the crazy-quilt pattern of domestic litigation in the United States, in which motions often can be made at any time and without prior permission of the court, and counsel are likely to be confronted with several motions—many of them, unfortunately, relating to discovery—at any one time.

5. Over the Long Term

The young lawyer may also wish to consider the longer-term rewards of a specialization in international commercial arbitration. But first, the drawbacks: When practiced in a large law firm

setting, international arbitration practice may not be as remuner-
ative as other specializations within the private practice of law.
Except in a few firms whose high-profile international arbitration
lawyers attract cases that last for years and generate millions of
dollars of fees annually, international arbitration practice is likely
to be derivative of the firm's transactional and commercial practices. This means that the lawyers handling the arbitrations are
often service partners for clients with whom other partners have
the primary relationships. Some of the largest global law firms
have questioned their commitment to international arbitration
practice, precisely because it is largely derivative of activity in
other more highly leveraged transactional and commercial practice groups. If your career focus turns to service as an arbitrator,
rewards may well be greater outside a large-firm environment, as
the economic mandate to generate work for other lawyers is eliminated, not to mention the conflicts of interest that might prevent
you from accepting available appointments.

I believe the nonmonetary rewards of international arbitration
practice are considerable, at least when compared to domestic dispute resolution practice. Significantly, you are joining a truly global
association of professionals in this field who have defined themselves, through various organizations and associations, formal and
informal, as the international arbitration bar. Each time you appear
as counsel in a case, there is a new opportunity to expand your professional reputation through the impression you make on opposing
counsel, and on each of the three members of the arbitral tribunal,
each of whom is likely to be a private practitioner whose impressions of your work will add luster to your global reputation. By the
time you have acted as counsel in your tenth international arbitration, you will have appeared before 30 international arbitrators
from all corners of the globe, done battle with many of the best
law firms in the world, engaged and worked with co-counsel and
experts who are among the foremost practitioners in the field—
and your own reputation should indeed be global! Add to this your
participation in conferences on international arbitration, your contributions to publications, and your own service as an arbitrator
and as a member of various committees and associations, and you
should have the opportunity to develop the kind of extensive net-

work of personal and professional contacts that is, in a sense, its own reward (not to mention a source of referrals that should help you to build a substantial practice).

E. Advice on Career Preparation

What, then, are the specific career initiatives that the aspiring international arbitration practitioner should take, beginning in law school and going forward? Here is a nonexhaustive list:

- *Consider obtaining an advanced law degree in international law and/or comparative law from a law school outside the United States,* at the same time perfecting your skills in a second language. International arbitration procedures are an amalgam of common law and civil law procedures, and often they are applied by arbitral tribunals in which common law and civil law traditions are each represented. Further, your ability to be an effective advocate for your clients in international arbitration will ultimately depend on your ability to communicate effectively with arbitrators from different legal and cultural traditions. Accordingly, training to be a comparativist at an early stage of your career will stand you in good stead later on.

- *Do not pass up the opportunities, if they are available to you, to serve in judicial clerkship positions within the U.S. federal system.* Bear in mind that, later on in your career when you are being evaluated as a potential counsel in an international arbitration case, foreign and American clients, will want to quickly assess your pedigree as an American trial lawyer. For the same reason, if you have an opportunity to serve in a prosecuting position in a U.S. Attorney's office, seize it.

- *Seek a governmental or judicial position specifically involved with international law or international dispute resolution.* A clerkship on an international arbitral tribunal, such as the Iran-U.S. Claims Tribunal, is one example. Serving in the Office of the Legal Adviser in the U.S. Department of

State is another. Opportunities for up-close exposure to international dispute resolution also exist within a variety of international organizations, including UN–related organizations such as the Geneva-based World Intellectual Property Organization (WIPO), which sponsors international arbitrations, and the Vienna-based UN Commission on International Trade Law (UNCITRAL), which is among the most active organizations in the world in the study of policy issues relating to international arbitration. You also may wish to consider service as staff counsel at the International Chamber of Commerce (ICC) International Court of Arbitration, based in Paris, which remains one of the world's most active institutional administrators of international arbitrations. Counsel at the ICC Secretariat are generally young lawyers with an interest in international arbitration. These positions are essentially apprenticeship positions with heavy administrative responsibility, but they offer the opportunity to participate in the selection of arbitrators and in the important work of the ICC Court in the management of ICC arbitrations.

- *Consider beginning your career in private practice in a foreign office of a U.S. law firm, or the office of a foreign law firm, which has an extensive specialized practice in international arbitration,* and in particular is the home to one or more practitioners who frequently serve as presiding arbitrators in complex international commercial arbitrations. Working with such a mentor, you will have an opportunity equivalent to that of a judicial law clerk in the U.S. system to master the facts, evidence, and applicable law; research the legal issues; and participate in the drafting of awards. With the same mentor, you are likely to serve as co-counsel in challenging, complex international arbitration cases; assist in preparing articles for publication; and appear as a speaker in international conferences on international commercial arbitration.

- *Be a joiner early in your career, volunteering your time and effort to various professional associations* (in exchange, implicitly, for exposure of your name and your talent). Be involved in the international arbitration committee of the ABA Section of International Law and Practice. Seek membership in the Institute for Transnational Arbitration, and attend its annual conference. Certainly, join the international arbitration committees of your local and state bar associations. Become a member of the International Bar Association, and in particular its Committee D, which focuses on international dispute resolution. Seek to become a Fellow of the Chartered Institute of Arbitrators, which is based in the United Kingdom and has branches in North America and generally throughout the British Commonwealth. The Chartered Institute offers fast-track fellowship courses for experienced professionals, which are generally intensive sessions over a period of several days, including oral evaluation and written examination.

- *Do superb legal work.* The international arbitration bar is a fluid and highly interconnected worldwide network. Particularly because members of this community are constantly in touch with one another concerning the selection of arbitrators, experts, and counsel, this is a branch of the bar in which the participants are uniquely undergoing constant and intensive peer evaluation. This may seem like advice to do things the old-fashioned way, but it remains true that the essential element of your long-range business development plan is your reputation for excellence.

- *Read the literature in the field regularly.* You should subscribe to the *ICCA Yearbook*, the *Journal of International Arbitration, Arbitration International, Mealey's International Arbitration Report*, the *ICC Bulletin*, and the *American Review of International Arbitration*. Find a number of Web sites that focus on international arbitration, and know how to navigate them to find rules, analyses, and bibliographies. Useful sites include those maintained by major international arbitration institutions, such as the WIPO, the ICC, and the LCIA, www.internationaladr.com, and sites of major publishing houses in the field, such as Kluwer Law Publishing.

- *Seek to have your name included in the lists of arbitrators of major international arbitration institutions*: the AAA, ICC,

LCIA, WIPO, Stockholm Chamber of Commerce, Hong Kong International Arbitration Center, Singapore International Arbitration Center, and the British Columbia International Arbitration Center. Eventually, opportunities for service as an arbitrator will begin to come your way. You can cross-fertilize your practice as counsel and as arbitrator. Each should nourish the other.

F. Where the Road Leads

So where might you find yourself after 20 years in practice, if you follow the sage advice given here? I cannot precisely tell you because, as I stated at the outset, I was a latecomer to the world of international commercial arbitration. I have been fortunate to secure several appointments as an arbitrator, such that about 40 percent of my practice now consists of service as an arbitrator. I have had the good fortune to serve as counsel in several complex, high-stakes, high-profile international commercial arbitrations. I have had the privilege of pleading on behalf of my clients before some of the most illustrious international arbitrators in the world. I have had international commercial arbitrations pending on three continents at one time, none of which was North America. I have represented clients from Europe, North America, and South America. I have had the privilege of working in close collaboration with expert witnesses of foreign and international law who have truly extraordinary legal minds and also are genuinely outstanding people. I have a network of friends and professional contacts that nearly spans the globe—and, with the benefit of e-mail, the ability to keep up with them on a daily basis.

Part 3

Public Sector

Practicing International Criminal Law

11

by Daryl A. Mundis[1]

A. Introduction

On July 7, 2000, Duško Sikirica, a former police officer in Prijedor, Bosnia and Herzegovina, entered pleas of not guilty to two counts of genocide, three counts of crimes against humanity, and two counts of violations of the laws or customs of war for his alleged role as commander of the Keraterm prison camp in northwestern Bosnia and Herzegovina. Although not a senior-level political leader in the conflict that consumed the former Yugoslavia in the early 1990s, Sikirica—who first appeared in court with his arm in a sling and with a broken nose, both allegedly inflicted when elite British troops snatched him from his home in the early morning

---

[1] The views expressed here are solely those of the author and are not to be imputed to the United Nations or the International Criminal Tribunal for former Yugoslavia.

of June 25, 2000—was allegedly one of countless other individuals who turned on their neighbors to kill or drive them away. He had his day in court, judged by the international community for his role in a conflict that the Security Council deemed to be such a threat to international peace and security that an international criminal tribunal was established to try those responsible for serious violations of international humanitarian law in the former Yugoslavia. I was one of the prosecutors trying the case against Sikirica and two other accused.

B. The Emerging International Criminal Law System

As recently as a decade ago, there were virtually no full-time practitioners of international criminal law. This is not to imply that lawyers were not engaged in transnational criminal matters, such as extradition or the occasional high-profile trial of individuals charged with acts of international terrorism or drug trafficking. But from the post–World War II Nuremberg and Tokyo trials until the establishment of the International Criminal Tribunal for the former Yugoslavia (ICTY) in 1993 or the International Criminal Tribunal for Rwanda (ICTR) in 1994, there were no international courts trying individuals alleged to have committed grave breaches of international law.

More recent developments suggest that international criminal law will continue to expand in the next few years and may well be the largest growth area for careers in public international law. For example, the International Criminal Court (ICC) is now fully functioning, as is the Special Court for Sierra Leone and the Iraqi Special Tribunal. The Extraordinary Chambers in the Courts of Cambodia will try the surviving leaders of the Khmer Rouge. It is also likely that a Tribunal will be established to prosecute persons responsible for the killing of former Lebanese Prime Minister Rafiq Hariri and 22 other individuals. As this list of courts indicates, notwithstanding the establishment of the ICC, the international community still has the option of establishing additional ad hoc international criminal tribunals.

This chapter explores opportunities and suggests possible directions for careers in this burgeoning field. At the outset, two important points should be kept in mind. First, the developing system of international criminal justice is focused on several core crimes: genocide, crimes against humanity, war crimes, and the still-undefined crime of aggression. The delegates who negotiated the Treaty of Rome establishing the ICC intentionally disregarded other serious international crimes, such as drug trafficking, terrorism, and money laundering, preferring to leave the prosecution of such crimes to national authorities. Second, there are career opportunities in federal and state court systems for individuals interested in these types of crime, although few government offices have large staffs devoted to prosecuting such crimes. Such opportunities are beyond the scope of this chapter.

The existing ad hoc international criminal tribunals (the ICTY and ICTR) are the primary focus of this chapter, because they are currently fully functional and will probably serve as the model for any future ad hoc tribunals. The types of career opportunities that are available at the ICC and the other international criminal institutions are similar to those at the ICTY and ICTR.

C.   The Structure of the ICTY and the Functions of Its Lawyers

Pursuant to the statutes of both the ICTY and ICTR, they are composed of three organs—Chambers, Registry, and the Office of the Prosecutor (OTP). Both the Registry and the OTP employ a substantial number of lawyers. The Chambers technically consist of the judges only; the lawyers who support the judges are staff members of the Registry. Although the two tribunals share a common basic structure (with minor differences), the discussion that follows is based on the ICTY.

As organs of the Security Council, the ICTY and ICTR follow the personnel policies of the UN; consequently, lawyers at the tribunals hold several different titles, based on experience and staffing requirements. Senior legal officers (or, in the OTP, senior trial lawyers) generally possess at least 12 years of professional experience. Legal officers generally have at least eight years of professional experience, while associate legal officers must usually have a minimum of three years. In the current structure, neither ad hoc tribunal has any positions at the assistant legal officer level (entry-level legal positions).

1. Chambers

Trials before the ad hoc tribunals are conducted without juries before trial chambers consisting of three judges, no two of whom are from the same country. Both tribunals have three trial chambers. In addition, both tribunals share a five-judge appeals chamber as a means of harmonizing the jurisprudence of the tribunals. Each judge is assigned one associate legal officer, and each chamber as a whole has two associate legal officers, one legal officer, and one senior legal officer (two for the appeals chamber). Thus, the Chambers Legal Support Unit (of the Registry) has about 32 lawyers.

These lawyers perform a variety of functions and tasks that are similar to the duties of law clerks in the U.S. system. This system is based more on the European model, whereby clerking for a judge may be a lifelong career. The senior legal officers thus have a great deal of responsibility and perform a variety of functions, such as overseeing depositions. More junior lawyers undertake legal research and assist with the drafting of orders, decisions, and judgments.

2. Registry

The Registry, which provides administrative support to the ad hoc tribunals, employs about a dozen lawyers who work on a variety of issues, including enforcement of sentences, relations between the tribunal and the host state, and other matters of general international law. The Registry has three lawyers assigned to the Office of Legal Aid, which administers the provision of high-quality legal representation to indigent accused and assists defense counsel with administrative matters. Finally, the Registry has one lawyer assigned to the Office of Public Information Services to assist with legal queries from the media and the public.

3. OTP

The Office of the Prosecutor employs the largest number of law-yers at both ad hoc tribunals. Under the current structure, there is one prosecutor for both the ICTY and ICTR. She has one deputy prosecutor responsible for each tribunal. As with the common appeals chamber, this structure permits greater harmonization between the prosecutorial policies at both ad hoc tribunals.

The OTP has approximately 60 lawyers in The Hague. As in many national police forces (such as the FBI), a significant number of the investigators have law degrees, although technically they are not working as lawyers, hence their role in the prosecution of cases will not be discussed further. The OTP is composed of two primary divisions, prosecutions and investigations, with several smaller units, such as the legal advisory section and the appeals section.

a. Prosecutions The prosecution division consists of about 50 trial lawyers, who are allocated to two functional sections: the trial section and the team legal officer and co-counsel units. Eight senior trial lawyers, each assisted by a trial section legal officer, form the backbone of the trial section. These lawyers are responsible for prosecuting cases, with the assistance of lawyers from the team legal officer and co-counsel units. As a general rule, the trial section legal officers assist the senior trial lawyers with written pleadings and drafting motions and responses to defense motions, although those with advocacy experience may appear and examine and cross-examine witnesses.

b. Investigations While the trial section lawyers spend the bulk of their time in court, moving from one case to the next as the cases are ready for trial, the team legal officers and lawyers from the co-counsel unit work closely with the investigators to develop the cases and move them through the pretrial stage. Once the accused is in custody and the trial chamber places the case on the docket, these lawyers assume the role of co-counsel, working directly under the supervision of the senior trial lawyer assigned to the case. These lawyers must be skilled at providing succinct yet accurate legal advice on investigative matters, including search-and-seizure issues. They also must be experienced in the art of questioning witnesses and victims and interrogating the accused. In short, the senior trial lawyers are highly experienced criminal litigators, and the co-counsel are experts on the case to be tried, based on their long experience in working with the evidence and witnesses throughout the period of investigation and pretrial workup.

c. **Legal Advisory Section and Appeals Unit** The legal advisory section, which consists of eight lawyers, provides critical support with respect to substantive issues of international humanitarian law and comparative legal analysis. The appeals unit, consisting of six lawyers, handles all legal issues arising during the course of either interlocutory appeals or appeals on the merits. Lawyers from both of these sections must have very strong research and writing skills, as well as a thorough knowledge of the applicable substantive and procedural law.

4. Defense Counsel

Finally, the practice of international criminal law also includes defense counsel. Pursuant to Article 21(4)(d) of the ICTY Statute, the accused has an absolute right to counsel of his or her own choosing. In the event the accused is unable to afford counsel, he or she is provided legal assistance at no cost to him or her. The Registry maintains a list of defense counsel eligible for assignment to defend indigent accused. Moreover, the lawyer must speak at least one of the two official languages of the tribunal (English or French) and must be willing to be assigned to represent any indigent suspect or accused. A lawyer who does not speak one of the official languages but speaks the native language of the suspect or accused may be admitted to the list at the request of a suspect or accused where the interests of justice so demand. Under the relevant directives on the assignment of counsel, an indigent accused also may be entitled to co-counsel and an investigator at no cost.

D.   The Pros and Cons of Life Inside the ICTY

Numerous professional and personal benefits arise from practicing international criminal law, particularly the opportunity for professional growth. This is the cutting edge of the law, and it provides endless opportunities to deal with issues of first impression, necessitating creative lawyering and problem solving. Because the Rules of Procedure and Evidence are a unique hybrid of common law and civil traditions, practice before the ad hoc tribunals presents educational challenges, forcing the practitioner to look at the law from different perspectives. Also, because we rely to a greater extent than most national systems on a comparative approach to the law, there are ample opportunities to learn about foreign criminal procedure.

From a personal point of view, most of us take great pride in the importance of the work we pursue. It is immensely gratifying to be a small part of reconciling the parties to the conflict in the former Yugoslavia, and working with victims and witnesses can be empowering. Most of us truly enjoy working in a multicultural institution, where most of the world's states are represented. There are travel opportunities for interviewing witnesses and collecting evidence. The benefits package is quite generous, although it cannot really be compared to the financial rewards of practicing with a big law firm.

These same advantages present certain drawbacks. Practicing international criminal law is not for the faint of heart. By definition, the crimes that are prosecuted at the ad hoc tribunals are serious and often involve mass killings, rape, and other offenses involving multiple victims. Working on the same case for months on end can take a psychological toll. As is the case with other types of litigation, the hours can be quite long, particularly during trial. Although it is exciting at first, many lawyers grow weary of the frequent travel necessary to interview witnesses, gather evidence, and visit crime scenes. It may seem exotic to travel to distant lands in search of the truth, but the fact is that many lawyers quickly tire of the substandard accommodations and lack of infrastructure that are all too common in areas that are regularly visited. Finally, although the financial rewards are generous, they are significantly less than what an experienced litigator could earn in private practice. In fact, starting salaries for first-year associates with major New York firms are higher than the salaries earned by senior legal officers and trial lawyers at the ad hoc tribunals. All of these factors can take a toll on practitioners with families who may not fully appreciate the personal sacrifices required in this type of work. Balancing the pros and cons, it is clear that international criminal practice may not be for everyone, but this type of work can be addictive.

E. Some Practical Advice for Law Students

My own experience may be helpful to students contemplating a career in international criminal law. As an undergraduate, I studied international relations and Russian, which included a summer abroad in the Soviet Union. Once in law school, I studied international law as my primary focus but also took as many courses in criminal law and procedure as my law school offered. While at law school, I joined several groups, including the American Society of International Law and Amnesty International. After passing the bar, I joined the U.S. Navy and was a criminal litigator for nearly six years, including two and a half years in a foreign country.

Following my discharge, I decided to pursue an LL.M. in international law. While studying, I attended as many conferences as possible, always bringing copies of my résumé with me. While attending one such conference, I made an effort to meet ICTY President Gabrielle Kirk McDonald. After exchanging pleasantries, she asked for a copy of my résumé, which I readily provided. Within a few months, and before I actually received the LL.M., I accepted a position in President McDonald's Chambers. When she retired from the ICTY 18 months later, I accepted a position with the ICTY Office of the Prosecutor, where I am now on the team prosecuting Dusko Sikirica.

There are as many routes into this career path as there are people practicing this type of law. However, all of the international criminal lawyers I have known have one thing in common: they all took full advantage of every opportunity that came their way. Those who are serious about a job in this area must maintain their focus on that goal and work to make it happen. The following are a few pointers that should help.

1. Law School

Many law schools today provide a wide range of international law subjects, and presumably anyone interested in a career in international criminal law would find many of these courses interesting. Other law schools, however, offer only an introductory course on international law, and a few do not even offer the basic course. The degree to which your law school offers courses in international law need not be a deterrent to your successful entry into this field, however, because the best advice for anyone contemplating a career in international criminal law is solid performance in law school.

Learning the basic skills necessary to be a good lawyer is essential for anyone aspiring to a career in international criminal law. This means learning to write clearly and succinctly, spot and address issues, and develop and frame an argument. Good research and advocacy skills—both oral and written—also are crucial. Participation in many moot courts or trial advocacy courses is a good idea. Joining the staff of an international or comparative law journal or submitting a note for publication also are wise moves.

All law students interested in this field should take the full package of courses available to all students interested in pursuing a career in criminal litigation. This includes criminal law, criminal procedure, and evidence. Advanced courses in due process or rights of the accused also should be taken, if possible. Choice of courses in law school should include international law, human rights law, and comparative law. Advanced courses or seminars in international humanitarian law, international criminal law, or similar courses should be taken if available.

2. Graduate School

Once the basics have been mastered, returning to law school to pursue an advanced degree may be a good idea. Earning an advanced law degree, such as the Masters of Law (LL.M.) in international law or even international criminal law, may be very helpful to those interested in a career in international criminal law and provide an edge over the competition. As previously discussed, the ad hoc tribunals have subject-matter jurisdiction over genocide, crimes against humanity, and violations of the laws or customs of war. Law school criminal law classes typically do not cover these offenses, and an understanding of the basics of these crimes will undoubtedly assist you in the process of job hunting in this field. Although some of the lawyers in the OTP lack this formal educational training, many others have earned such degrees, and given the stiff competition for positions, the more formal education you possess, the stronger your chances of being hired.

In many countries, students pursue the Bachelor of Laws (LL.B.) degree as the first college degree out of high school. Thus, unlike their U.S. counterparts, the first law degree is not pursued after the completion of a basic undergraduate degree. Many of these students then pursue a specialized LL.M. in international law immediately after graduation from college, then go on to earn doctorates in international law before entering the job market. Because of this difference in how lawyers are trained throughout the world, an advanced law degree may be helpful in landing the position desired.

Many law schools offer an LL.M. in international law, and a few even offer a highly specialized LL.M. in international criminal law. Such training will prove invaluable as you master the substantive law necessary to be an effective international criminal litigator. Moreover, many of the faculties offering advanced law degrees in international criminal law are located overseas, such as in the United Kingdom or the Netherlands. By pursuing such a degree program, you can also take advantage of studying and living abroad.

3. Study or Living Abroad

Many law schools and other higher-education institutions offer summer, semester, and/or year abroad programs. These programs should be seriously considered, because they offer the opportunity to learn about new legal cultures and languages. Study abroad programs also are great ways to meet other students with similar interests. The friendships and connections made during the course of such programs may last a lifetime.

4. Practical Experience

Because there are few, if any, entry-level positions in this career field, the best career advice is to gain as much criminal or appellate litigation experience as possible. The strongest candidates are those with excellent oral and written advocacy skills and the ability to work closely with investigators in developing a case. Good written and spoken communications skills are essential, as is the ability to analyze complex factual situations. Trials at the ad hoc tribunals tend to be rather lengthy, with numerous exhibits and witnesses. For example, the Blaškic' trial lasted for 25 months. In terms of complexity and length of trial, the closest analogy to domestic trials is probably a prosecution under the RICO statute.

Virtually all lawyers practicing international criminal law began their careers practicing criminal law in their national jurisdictions. The skills learned as a young lawyer in the office of the local district attorney or U.S. attorney are invaluable. Young lawyers in such offices are exposed to what criminal practice is all about and usually are assigned a large number of cases, forcing them to juggle many legal issues simultaneously. The procedural issues that are confronted—evidentiary matters, due process problems, search-and-seizure issues, and substantive legal questions—are crucial training for any lawyer who wants to pursue a career in international criminal law.

Working in a foreign country and in a multicultural environment with people from different legal backgrounds is enjoyable. Because teams of lawyers work on all cases, the ability to work closely with others and respect their point of view is a definite asset. Finally, a keen awareness of current events in the world is a big plus. The headlines of a conflict in a far-off land today may be the basis of a lawyer's practice tomorrow.

5. Internships

Several internships may lead to full-time paid positions in international criminal law. For example, interns generally perform substantive legal work in all three organs of both ad hoc tribunals. However, there are slight drawbacks to these programs. First, they are unpaid and generally require a commitment of four to six months.

Second, the intern is forbidden under UN regulations from applying for a paid position for six months following the end of the internship. Thus, more than one year will elapse between the commencement of the internship and any resulting paid employment. Third, because law students from many countries also apply, the competition consists of students who have already completed their LL.M. (and may be working on their Ph.D.). Nevertheless, an internship can be a very rewarding experience, and for most interns, the experience confirms that the practice of international criminal law is what they want to pursue.

For more information on employment or internship opportunities at these institutions, the following Web sites are helpful:

ICTY: http://www.un.org/icty/pratical-e/index.htm

ICC: http://www.icc-cpi.int/recruitment.html

ICTR: http://69.94.11.53/default.htm

Special Court for Sierra Leone:
     http://www.sc-sl.org/

Khmer Rouge Tribunal:
     http://www.eccc.gov.kh/english/job_opportunity.aspx

Additional opportunities may be found by clicking the "Legal Affairs" or "Jurists" tabs at the UN employment Web site:
     https://jobs.un.org/Galaxy/Release3/vacancy/vacancy.aspx

6. Language Training

Both ad hoc tribunals use English and French as their official languages, although the witnesses are likely to speak Bosnian, Croatian, Serbian (at the ICTY), or Kinyarwanda (at the ICTR). The ICC, however, will use the official languages of the UN (Arabic, Chinese, English, French, Russian, and Spanish), and witnesses appearing before that court are likely to speak a wide range of languages. Thus, it is difficult to determine which language is the most likely to help you get the position you want.

Unless one has a gift for languages, is very diligent in language studies, or has the opportunity to live or study abroad for a considerable period of time, fluency in a foreign language will probably not be achieved. Do not let this deter you from making the effort to learn a new language, however. Learning a foreign language has numerous benefits and will always open doors for the student who takes full advantage of the opportunity. In addition to promoting cross-cultural communication, language skills help develop different ways of thinking and provide an edge in a competitive environment.

7. Networking

Opportunities abound for networking with professionals in the field, and this may be an important means of learning of job openings. Given the sharp rise in interest in international criminal law, there are typically panels on the subject at most annual meetings of professional groups. For example, the ABA's Section of International Law and Practice, the American Society of International Law, and the International Association of Prosecutors typically offer panels and discussion groups addressing these issues during their regular meetings. The ABA Section of International Law and Practice has several committees for individuals interested in a career in international criminal law, including the International Criminal Law Committee and the International Courts Committee. Several nongovernmental organizations, such as Amnesty International, Human Rights Watch, and the Lawyers Committee for Human Rights, also are quite active in issues that interest practicing international criminal lawyers. Joining such organizations and actively participating in their meetings will provide a familiarity with the key players in the field. The publications of and internship opportunities at such organizations also can be helpful to those who would like to pursue a career in international criminal law.

F. Conclusion

The challenges of working in the dynamic area of international criminal law are great, and the rewards are even greater. However, the work is not easy and, frankly, can be depressing at times, because it focuses on some of the evil acts of humanity. Dealing with victims and criminals can be emotionally draining. Nevertheless, most of us engaged in this line of work take a great deal of pride and satisfaction in knowing that our work is of great importance to victims and their families, witnesses, and the international community as a whole. If we can play a small role in reconciling past international conflicts—and deterring future atrocities—then that is a true privilege.

An International Judge in Kosovo

12

by Hon. Marilyn J. Kaman

A. Introduction

My career in international law began unexpectedly. As I sat at in my office as a state-court trial judge in Hennepin County, Minnesota, a succinct e-mail appeared on my computer, from federal Judge Jack Tunheim, who had recently returned from Kosovo and who had been instrumental in rebuilding the judiciary in Kosovo after the 1999 conflict ended. The e-mail sent to all Minnesota state-court trial judges asked, "Would any Minnesota trial judge be interested in serving as an International Judge in Kosovo?" and contained the following announcement:

Field Mission Vacancy Notice

Field Mission Vacancy Notice
EXTERNAL/INTERNAL

Vacancy #: MIK/01-010-second issue   Deadline: 21 March 2002
Post Title: International Judge
Post Level: P-5/D-1
Location: Pristina, Kosovo
 	
………
 	
Duties and Responsibilities:
Under the overall supervision of the Director of the Department of Justice, the incumbent serves as an international judge in one of the five District Courts in Kosovo or in the Supreme Court of Kosovo, based in Pristina. In this role, the incumbent shall:
    Select, with a view to investigate or adjudicate, serious criminal cases within the jurisdiction of the courts of their assignment, including cases of genocide, war crimes, organized crime, murder, terrorism, ethnically motivated offences, trafficking in drugs and human beings, and smuggling of weapons and ammunition.
    Provide legal support and advice to the Department of Justice on criminal legal issues and the application of international human rights standards in Kosovo. Assist in UNMIK's overall efforts of strengthening the judiciary and establishing the rule of law in Kosovo. Participate and promotes institutional- and capacity-building efforts by UNMIK of the Kosovo judiciary at both the regional and provincial level. Perform any other duties that fall within the jurisdiction of judges as set out in the applicable law and UNMIK Regulations.
 	
Qualifications:
Advanced university degree in law from a recognized university. Minimum of 20 years of relevant experience including 10 years handling criminal law cases as a professional judge in a court equivalent to the District Court in Kosovo or higher. Knowledge of the civil law system and/or the applicable law in Kosovo preferred. Familiarity with international human rights standards and legal principles.

The notice seemed clear enough. It called for a judge who could adjudicate criminal cases and provide support on criminal legal issues. The qualifications seemed to be tailor-made to my own professional experience. I first entered the field of criminal law as a public defender in Hennepin County, Minnesota, which handles a greater volume of criminal cases than any other county in the state. By the time of my appointment to the district court bench six years later, I had tried dozens of jury cases and understood trial practice. This experience in criminal cases was reinforced by 12 years as a state-court trial judge, during which time I had encountered virtually every criminal case type within Minnesota's Criminal Code. Implicit in the notice also was a willingness to travel and to encounter the unknown. With my travel and education in the former Soviet Union in 1971, another piece of the puzzle was in place. By answering that e-mail, my career in international law was launched. My application (and the application of three other Minnesota trial court judges) was accepted. On November 17, 2002, I boarded a plane for Kosovo and became a participant in the post-war reconstruction process.

B. United Nations Mission in Kosovo

1. Some Background

The social fabric of Kosovo was torn apart by the region's ethnic strife during the 1980s and the 1990s. The conflict, between the Kosovar Serbs and Kosovar Albanians, dates back to the year 1389, with an Ottoman Empire victory at Kosovo Polje/Fushë Kosovë, on the outskirts of present-day Pristina. With the death of Yugoslav President Josef Tito in 1980, the uneasy truce keeping the republics of Yugoslavia together—as well as ethnic rivalries—unraveled. Serbian leader Slobodan Milosevic rallied ethnic Serbs at Kosovo Polje/Fushë Kosovë in 1987 by declaring, "No one should dare to beat you!" During the 1990s, Kosovar Albanian judges and police were dismissed from their posts, and schools for Kosovar Albanian children were closed.

A campaign to expel the Kosovar Albanian population from Kosovo was implemented. Newspapers across the world carried pictures of the forced exodus. NATO intervened on March 23, 1999, and the conflict ended 87 days later. On June 10, 1999, the United Nations Mission in Kosovo (UNMIK) was created by UN Security Council Resolution 1244. UNMIK's mandate was to act as the interim and transitional civilian administration for the region. Part of that mandate would be to maintain civil law and order, including establishment of the rule of law.

In 2000, UNMIK asked international judges and prosecutors to participate in Kosovo's judicial processes in order to ensure the independence and impartiality of the judiciary and the proper administration of justice. The continuing distrust of one ethnicity toward the other adversely affecting trial outcomes after June 1999 required this action.

2. *Broadening Professional Knowledge and Expertise*

The role of a judge in Kosovo, as I experienced it, was different from that of a state-court trial judge in the United States. The judicial system in Kosovo had its origins in the European civil law system (a new Criminal Code and Code of Criminal Procedure have since been adopted, modifying Kosovo's long-standing legal system). In addition to being a trial judge, I was called on to be an investigative judge, assuming a quasi-prosecutorial role by investigating crimes that had occurred and questioning witnesses and possible suspects.

The Field Vacancy Notice was accurate in the cases assigned to International Judges: war crimes, organized crime, murder, terrorism, ethnically motivated offenses, trafficking in drugs and human beings, and smuggling of weapons and ammunition. While in Kosovo, in addition to investigative hearings, I either was a presiding judge or panel judge on three trial panels. The war crimes case involved a defendant of Montenegrin origin accused of committing crimes against Kosovar Albanians in villages of the Pec/Pejë during 1998 and 1999. Trial began in late January 2003 and concluded on June 26, 2003. The trial panel of three judges (two international judges and one professional Kosovar judge) found the defendant guilty of 7 counts of war crimes and acquitted him of 23 counts of war crimes. The second lengthy case involved charges of murder against two Kosovar Albanians accused of killing another Kosovar Albanian man for allegedly collaborating with Serbian authorities. The killing occurred on February 18, 1998 (before recognition of the existence of an internal conflict in Kosovo). The trial panel of five judges (International Presiding Judge, professional Kosovar judge, three lay judges) convicted one defendant and acquitted the other.

The work to be done required not only learning the civil law system, but also integrating and applying several bodies of law as well: the Criminal Code for the Socialist Federal Republic of Yugoslavia, the Criminal Procedural Code for SFRY, the Serbian Criminal Code of 1989 (selected articles), the Kosovo Criminal Code, the Kosovo Code of Minor Offenses, international treaties, and principles of international law and international human rights.

For the next nine months as an International Judge in Kosovo, I delved into investigations, heard trials, and researched the applicable law. The process of judging in a civil law context sometimes required putting aside my common law approach to legal issues. What at first appeared to require a certain result, upon further examination called for a different result or approach. In short, my experience was a legal education by immersion that has greatly expanded my professional knowledge and expertise.

3. Professional and Personal Challenges

The professional and personal challenges that most quickly come to mind are summed up with the words *cold* and *intimidation*. The sheer cold of living without heat and electricity much of the day made an impression even on this hardy Minnesotan. Intimidation was a real message sent to both the international and the local Kosovar judges, by those who do not want the rule of law to prevail in Kosovo.

a. The Cold Journal entry, February 18, 2003:

> *It was cold in court today. We didn't have electricity for much*
>
> *of the session. We could see our breath in the courtroom.*
>
> *Luckily I put on an ankle-length skirt when I got dressed this*
>
> *morning. While listening to the testimony in the courtroom,*

I looked down at my legs, and realized that underneath my

skirt was my long wool underwear that I have been using as

pajamas. My down coat was draped over my legs. I looked at

the defendant, and he looked cold and forlorn. The witnesses

who came to testify also looked cold and forlorn.

Two of my trial cases extended over a period of months and involved some thorny legal issues (war crimes prosecution). That being said, what would have been routine case-processing issues at home became hurdles to overcome: Would the witnesses in the outlying villages receive their subpoenas on time? Would any witnesses show up for court today? How could we contact village witnesses and tell them we were running behind? Was there any money with which to pay the witness fee? Would the court's backup generator work, or not? If not, how long would the court recorder's laptop function without electricity? Would the courthouse telephone land lines function on any given day? How cold should the courtroom be, before court is cancelled?

I am routinely asked what kinds of cases I heard, as well as the volume of my caseload. "Was it one case per day? One case per week? Do you mean you only tried three cases and you were in Kosovo for over seven months?" People are polite, but incredulous. The Field Mission Vacancy Notice did not draw attention to the word *mission*. Being "in mission" means doing without the conveniences taken for granted at home, such as reliable heat, light, and communication means. By Minnesota standards, the winter in Kosovo was not cold—the coldest temperature was in the 20s Fahrenheit. Without reliable electricity in Kosovo, however, that mild winter became very cold, indeed. The sheer cold affected the way we did our work, as well as the way we lived.

b. Intimidation As I drove to work in Kosovo on January 23, 2003, I approached the parking lot and saw yellow "Police Line Do Not Cross" tape extending around the perimeter of my building. A rocket-propelled grenade had been fired the night before into the Regional Police Headquarters in Pec/Pejë, Kosovo. This building housed offices of all Pec/Pejë international judges, international prosecutors, international interpreters, UN support staff, and international civilian police. About one week later, a Kosovar Albanian judge was severely beaten outside his home in Prizren by persons unknown. One theory regarding the first incident is that displeasure was being expressed for a verdict rendered in December by my international colleague from Uganda. One theory regarding the second incident is that the local judge was too enthusiastic in his support of the prosecution of certain criminal elements.

Whatever the cause, the intended effect was clear: to create a climate of fear affecting judicial decision making. Once fear enters the equation, a judicial outcome can be dictated by politically or personally expedient considerations. While I was in Kosovo, two armed bodyguards accompanied me wherever I went. My Kosovar judicial colleagues did not have any protection. I often put myself in their shoes: Would I be able to make the correct decision, without protection and in a society filled with ethnic distrust, intimidation, and fear? It was not an easy question to ask myself. It is even more difficult to come up with an answer.

The cold and intimidation were only two of the challenges faced while I was in Kosovo. Yet, each challenge also was an opportunity for learning, both professional and personal.

C.   Your Own Career in International Law

My mission to Kosovo ended in June 2003 at the end of my leave of absence and return to work as a state-court trial judge. In a real sense, however, my career in international law was just beginning. If you are considering a career in international law, the following sections provide some suggestions for you.

1.   Career or Calling?

The word *career* most often calls up the connotation of a full-time occupation, established early in one's professional life. I now know that this one definition is not controlling and, in fact, may be a definition that, if adhered to, limits one's professional experience and opportunity. It may be better to note the dictionary definition of *career*: "a profession for which one trains and which is undertaken as a permanent calling" (Merriam-Webster). You can begin your career either while you are in law school, early thereafter, or sometime later in your professional career. The timing doesn't matter. What does matter is that if you are interested in international law, you should begin with the activity or subject matter that interests you. I have done reading, audited law school courses, joined professional organizations focusing on international law, written articles, and traveled as a delegation member to foreign countries. Through these activities, I consider myself to have a permanent calling in international law, one to which I am committed and about which I am most excited.

2. *Legal Education*

As is clear from what I have written, my legal education in international law developed backward. Instead of learning international law in advance, I learned by immersion once on the ground. It was a challenging process to learn, assimilate, and apply a new body of law all at once. On this issue, I would recommend learning ahead of time and getting all of the knowledge that you can.

If you are in law school, this means taking advantage of whatever international law courses your school has to offer. Take the introductory course in international law, and then follow up with courses in international criminal law, international humanitarian law, international human rights law, and advanced seminars on these subjects. Learn all you can about the UN, its history, programs, and international law initiatives. If comparative law courses are offered, take them. The more you know about major legal systems, adherence to treaties, and their implementation, the better trained you will be.

You also should not overlook the obvious: If you want to work in the arena of international criminal law, you should develop a solid foundation of litigation experience and criminal law expertise. This includes criminal law, criminal procedure, and evidence (beginning and advanced). Good oral and written advocacy skills are essential, and experience in moot court competition would be a definite asset. Finally, if your school offers legal advice clinics where you can appear in court (under the supervision of licensed attorneys) representing actual clients, you should consider enrolling in these clinics. Responding to the needs of clients, researching their legal problems, and finding solutions is far different from reading about it in textbooks. It is also excellent preparation for deciphering criminal issues in a litigation context in the future.

3. The Internet

Opportunities abound for careers in international law, both at home and abroad. If you are focusing on international court opportunities, each court has a Web site that will have "Job Recruitment" and/or internship opportunities. See the following court Web sites:

- The International Criminal Court (ICC) is an independent, permanent court that tries persons accused of the most serious crimes of international concern, namely genocide, crimes against humanity, and war crimes. The ICC is based on a treaty, joined by 104 countries. http://www.icc-cpi.int/
- The International Criminal Tribunal for the former Yugoslavia (ICTY) was established in 1993 in response to the threat to international peace and security, with the authority to prosecute and try grave breaches of the Geneva Conventions, genocide, and crimes against humanity; it currently is under a completion strategy targeted for 2010. http://www.un.org/icty/
- The International Criminal Tribunal for Rwanda (ICTR) was created in 1994 to prosecute persons responsible for genocide and other serious violations of international humanitarian law committed within Rwanda, as well as prosecution of Rwandan citizens committing crimes within neighboring states during the relevant period. http://69.94.11.53/default.htm
- The Extraordinary Chambers in the Courts of Cambodia was established in 2001 by a vote of the Cambodian National Assembly that enacted a law to create a court to try serious crimes committed during the Khmer Rouge regime from 1975 to 1979. This court is officially called the

Extraordinary Chambers in the Courts of Cambodia for the Prosecution of Crimes Committed during the Period of Democratic Kampuchea (Extraordinary Chambers or ECCC). This special new court was created by the government of Cambodia and the UN, and will apply international standards. http://www.eccc.gov.kh/english/default.aspx

- A Special Tribunal for Lebanon was established in November 2006 by the UN Security Council, which voted to establish a special tribunal to investigate the assassination of Rafik Hariri in 2005.

- The Office of the High Representative is an ad hoc international institution responsible for overseeing implementation of civilian aspects of the accord ending the war in Bosnia and Herzegovina, and under its auspices a War Crimes Chamber is operated. http://www.ohr.int/

4. *Networking*

Upon my return from Kosovo, I promptly flew to San Francisco for the ABA Annual Meeting and joined the Section of International Law. My initial focus was the UN International Institutions Committee. From that, I have gone on to become a Deputy Editor of *International Law News* and Co-Chair of the International Criminal Law Committee, and I have taken International Legal Exchange (ILEX) trips to The Hague, Ghana, Liberia, and Sierra Leone. The ABA Section of International Law has committees that will be of interest to you. By not only joining but actively participating in these committees, you will continue to learn new developments in international law and will meet the leaders in their respective fields.

Moreover, internships are sometimes available on a short-term basis, during which time you will be able to perform substantive legal work and gain direct practical experience. The internships may be unpaid and are generally from four to six months. The International Criminal Court, for example, has both Internship Placements and Visiting Professional Placements, depending on the stage of your career. By trying one of these short-term internships, you can gain direct experience while determining whether a career in international law is right for you.

If you are a state-court trial judge, determine whether your district has a judicial leave of absence policy. I had the good fortune to go to Kosovo because our Chief Justice, Governor, and district Chief Judges jointly implemented a judicial leave policy (without pay) for endeavors such as this. If your judicial district does not have a policy permitting you to take an unpaid leave of absence from your judicial duties, it would be a project worthwhile pursuing. As an international judge, you will find your professional horizons broadened and personal insights gained, while you foster the rule of law abroad.

5. Adaptability and Resilience

Doing the work of an international judge and living abroad requires a certain resilience and adaptability. If romantic notions come to mind, the reality is that this field requires a lot of hard work, under suboptimal conditions, and focuses on crimes that are some of the most horrific imagined. Yet what the work required of me is also what nourished me. Sitting with my colleagues in a small and bare courtroom in Kosovo, with only two desks, essential staff, a couple of guards, and counsel, it nevertheless was clear to me that this work was important to the world at large. It was tremendously satisfying to model the rule of law for the defendant, the victims, and the Kosovo judges and lawyers watching this process unfold. Working with my UN colleagues was an eminently gratifying experience, and one that has made a permanent impression on me.

D. Conclusion

After I returned home, I was asked what my experience in Kosovo was like. Here is my answer: Think of an adjective, any adjective at all. Whatever the adjective is, it likely applies to my experience in Kosovo. However, from my standpoint, the final adjective would have to be *extraordinary*. Being an International Judge in Kosovo was simply an extraordinary experience, fundamentally affecting my perspective on life and the law. If you are considering a career in international law, I highly encourage you to pursue this as your career calling.

The Practice of International Trade Law in the Public Sector

13

by Eleanor Roberts Lewis[1]

A. Introduction

Someday, as a young lawyer, you will have a difficult choice to make. Should you work for a private law firm, where you will represent specific paying clients, where the hours are almost always long, but for which the financial rewards are generally very high? Or should you enter public service, where you will

---

[1] I would like to thank Allyson L. Senie, a former senior counsel at the U.S. Department of Commerce, for her substantial assistance in the preparation of this chapter, particularly the section on lifestyle issues. I also would like to thank Pamela Jessen, formerly a paralegal at the Commerce Department, for her work on the summaries of international legal opportunities in federal agencies. The views expressed in this chapter are my own and not those of any other person or U.S. government agency.

earn a more modest income but have the opportunity to serve more than 300 million American citizens and enjoy a more balanced lifestyle?

After earning my J.D. at Georgetown University, I went to work as a staff lawyer for the U.S. Department of Housing and Urban Development (HUD). I initially chose the public sector because of my interest in the public policy aspects of law and because I hoped the federal government would provide a supportive environment for a mother with a newborn child. After two years at HUD, I received a good offer from a private law firm and decided to try it out. I learned many important things during my three years in private practice, including the discipline to focus on the needs of a particular client, but I missed being on the front lines of public policy issues, and I did not find law firms at that time to be very family-friendly. So I returned to HUD, this time as head lawyer for the Government National Mortgage Association and the public housing finance program.

In 1982, I was offered the opportunity to set up a new legal office at the U.S. Department of Commerce to focus on the market access and transactional aspects of international trade and investment. Until then, the existing international legal offices at Commerce concentrated primarily on the regulatory aspects of trade, such as export controls and antidumping/countervailing duties. I hesitated to accept the position, having practiced only project finance and other areas of real estate law for eight years. I had studied international law academically but had never practiced in the field outside the finance context. "A woman's response," said my mentor at the time. He noted that women often assume they must be expert in a field before applying for or accepting a job, whereas men generally assume they can learn on the job. Suggesting that any good lawyer could master any subject in a few months or even a few weeks, he advised that I buy some books on trade law and accept the position. I followed his advice, although it took more than a few months and a few books for me to become truly comfortable with such a major change in professional specialties.

It proved to be a worthwhile move. After I began work at the Commerce Department, I dealt almost daily with both interesting and important matters. Some of the legal problems and work environment issues in the public practice of trade law are similar to those found in private practice, but many are different in ways that may make a public-sector career particularly appealing. This chapter discusses specific examples of the substantive work, as well as personal considerations, involved in being an international trade lawyer in the public sector, concluding with a brief description of some federal agencies that employ international trade lawyers.

B.   Why Practice What They Teach?

Many of us now practicing international law took at least one course in college or law school on general international law, trade law, or comparative law. Even as a student, I realized that these subjects entailed an especially complex and even exotic mixture of legal and policy issues that were domestic, foreign, and multinational in scope. The practice of trade law in the public sector more than lives up to the intellectual expectations engendered by the academic environment. It also offers possibilities for travel and exposure to diverse cultures that I had not explored in school. Consider these illustrative examples from my own career.

1.   Trade Agreements

My most high-profile and exciting work involved being part of interagency teams that negotiated, interpreted, and enforced trade and investment agreements with foreign governments. During the course of my career in trade law, I worked on diverse, challenging assignments related to negotiation and implementation of the U.S.–Canada Free Trade Agreement and its successor, the North American Free Trade Agreement (NAFTA); the World Trade Organization (WTO) agreements; the U.S.–Japan Automotive Agreement; the Organization for Economic Cooperation and Development (OECD) Convention on Bribery; and the U.S.–Australia Free Trade Agreement; as well as bilateral investment treaties with such diverse countries as Poland, Tunisia, and Argentina.

The goal of NAFTA was the substantial elimination of trade and investment barriers among the United States, Canada, and Mexico, in order to create a market with almost 400 million consumers, almost $7 trillion in annual output, and more than $500 billion in annual trade. With approximately 1,000 pages of legal text and 1,000 pages of tariff schedules, much was riding on every word and number in NAFTA. In addition to fairly common provisions on tariff and customs matters, NAFTA for the first time covered in detail nontariff issues such as trade in services, intellectual property rights, and investment, as well as sanitary/phytosanitary measures (agricultural standards). Government lawyers played an important role in shaping NAFTA, which in turn strongly influenced the WTO negotiations that were under way at the same time. My work on NAFTA was not limited to technical legal issues; it also entailed contributions to policy development and representation of diverse U.S. agency and private-sector interests.

The OECD Convention on Bribery also will have an important impact on U.S. commercial interests. It has been estimated that U.S. firms have been losing many billions of dollars per year because their foreign competitors pay bribes to win foreign government business. Since 1977, U.S. firms have been prohibited from making such payments by the Foreign Corrupt Practices Act (FCPA). This convention, the product of almost eight years of discussion and negotiations, internationalizes the basic principle of the FCPA: no person may offer, promise, or give any money or other advantage to a foreign public official to obtain or retain business. In this convention, for which my office provided critical drafting and negotiating support, the governments of other developed countries agree to adopt the same high, anticorruption standard to which U.S. law holds U.S. companies in their international transactions.

2.   Trade-Related Legislation, Dispute Settlement, and Litigation

The negotiation of NAFTA, WTO, and numerous other trade and investment agreements requires extensive involvement by government lawyers. In addition, government lawyers play an essential role in the development and drafting of related legislation. For example, the bill drafted by the Executive Branch to implement NAFTA was about 450 pages long and was accompanied by a 260-page "statement of administrative action" to explain the provisions of the agreement and legislation. Although lawyers from the U.S. Trade Representative's Office take the lead in drafting such legislative documents (as they generally do in trade negotiations), lawyers from the Commerce Department and several other agencies are an essential part of the interagency team that produces the final product.

After trade agreements become effective, government lawyers continue to play an important role in assessing whether our foreign trading partners are complying with their obligations. When it seems these partners are not complying, Commerce Department lawyers assist in consultations with the foreign governments to encourage compliance. If consultations are unsuccessful, the lawyers advise on the application of domestic trade laws as well as assist the U.S. Trade Representative with the dispute settlement cases that may be brought under NAFTA and WTO.

Trade agreements are sometimes challenged in court, such as the litigation over the constitutionality of NAFTA.[2] Interesting issues also arise about the allocation of appropriate government roles in the commercial and foreign policy arenas. For example, in one of our cases, the Supreme Court decided that the state of Massachusetts did not have the right to institute unilateral economic sanctions against Burma when the U.S. federal government had already developed an elaborate framework to address human rights abuses by that country.[3] Although the Justice Department is responsible for filing the briefs and making the oral arguments in such cases, lawyers from Commerce and other affected U.S. agencies are extensively involved in the process.

3.   Advice and Advocacy for U.S. Exporters and Investors

The daily work of some lawyers at the Commerce Department is counseling U.S. firms and their lawyers about questions or problems that arise in foreign business transactions. Issues range from formation of contracts and hiring of agents/distributors to protection of intellectual property rights and settlement of commercial

---

[2] *Made in the USA Foundation v. U.S.*, 56 F. Supp. 2d 1226 (N.D. Ala. 1999), *appeal dismissed,* 242 F. 3rd 1300 (11th Cir. Ala 2001), *cert. denied, United Steelworkers v. U.S.*, 122 S. Ct. 613 (2001).

[3] *Crosby v. National Foreign Trade Council*, 530 U.S. 363 (2000).

disputes. The U.S. government also has an aggressive program to support U.S. firms bidding for foreign government contracts. The international government procurement market amounts to hundreds of billions of dollars per year. Many interesting and often complex legal and policy issues arise with respect to which companies and products the U.S. government should support and how that support should be offered.

4.   Technical Assistance for Foreign Countries

An exciting and gratifying role for lawyers at Commerce is to provide technical legal assistance to foreign governments trying to establish a market economy and seeking advice on how to develop the necessary underlying commercial legal structure. Generally, these countries are converting from a communist or other centralized economic system, but sometimes they are recovering from domestic turmoil. Examples of countries we have assisted include Russia, China, South Africa, Iraq, and most of the countries of Eastern Europe.

5.   Equal and Better Opportunities

The practice of international trade law with the U.S. government virtually guarantees inherently interesting and important assignments. It also offers other advantages: Because government offices almost always have more work than they can handle, young lawyers typically are given more responsibility earlier than they ordinarily would have it in a law firm. A government lawyer right out of law school can expect in the first year to have direct client contact and a relatively independent caseload, as well as opportunities to represent his or her office in interagency meetings. Within two years of employment, most international lawyers at the Commerce Department have participated in negotiations with foreign government officials.

In addition, the federal government takes seriously the legal requirement and public policy goal that women, minorities, and other disadvantaged persons be given an equal opportunity to succeed. For example, although women have constituted almost half of most law school classes for many years, only about 15 percent of the partners in private law firms are women. By contrast, women make up more than 25 percent of all government GS-15–level lawyers (equivalent in experience and stature to partners), and almost as high a percentage of government Senior Executive Service (SES) lawyers are women. (SES legal positions are similar to senior or managing partners in law firms.) The statistics for minority and disabled lawyers similarly reflect the more welcoming and upwardly mobile environment of the public sector.

C. Balancing Family and Work

What does all this talk about balancing family and work mean in real life? Start with the morning: Instead of just getting yourself up, dressed, fed, and out the door for your daily commute, it may be you plus one or two or more dependents. You may be caring for young children, an elderly live-in parent, or a sick family member who must be prepared for their daily routines as well. This usually entails getting them up, dressed, and fed before turning them over to a daytime caregiver. Whatever the scenario, you must build an extra hour or more into morning activities before turning your attention to work once you finally reach your desk. Now fast-forward through your day and picture the evening ritual of racing to leave the office to pick up your dependents from the daycare provider. Your colleagues have one more question, your boss needs one more item researched; you download the memo you have been working on to a CD, promising yourself you will return to it once the rest of the family is in bed. You answer the phone one last time and fly out of the office, late again.

Congress and the Executive Branch have become increasingly sensitized to the inherent stresses of balancing work and family. A major driving force behind this change is the increasing number of women who choose to or must work outside the home while continuing to shoulder major family responsibilities. Today more than 40 percent of women caring for children under three years old are working outside the home, and almost 80 percent of women with children ages 6 to 17 are in the labor force.

Another driving force is the realization by men that spending time actively assisting in the day-to-day activities of child rearing or caring for elderly or sick family members is important and may even be a necessity when both parents work. All of the male lawyers in my previous office at the Commerce Department had excellent credentials, and most have had jobs with first-rate private law firms. However, these bright, dedicated men, as well as the exceptional women lawyers in my office, chose public service not only for its interesting, important work, but also for the more balanced lifestyle it provides compared to private practice.

A balanced lifestyle does not always mean shorter hours. When a major project entails demanding deadlines, a government lawyer can work as long and travel as much as any private-sector lawyer. However, in a government legal office, there will rarely be the pressure to work late into the night or show up on the weekends just to compete and impress. Fortunately, the federal government has implemented several programs to help employees balance family and professional responsibilities.

1. Flexible Work Schedules

In 1994, the President issued a memorandum to executive agencies directing them to establish programs to support flexible, family-friendly work arrangements. Since then, federal employees have been able to choose part-time employment, job-sharing arrangements, telecommuting, and alternative work schedules permitting flexible hours and compressed workdays. Government studies show that these flexible workplace programs improve recruitment, lower absenteeism, and increase morale and retention of good employees.

2. Child Care

More than 110 federal child-care centers were operating in or near federal buildings in more than 30 states and the District of Columbia. The hours of operation at these centers vary, but almost 90 percent are open 11 or more hours per day. More than 90 percent also offer infant care, generally beginning at three months of age. All centers located in government-owned space must be accredited by the National Association for the Education of Young Children (NAEYC).

Federal child-care programs are attractive for many working parents, who can easily drop off and pick up children. In addition, they may be able to see their children during the workday. Most centers have an open drop-in policy, affording mothers the important opportunity to continue nursing after returning to work or allowing parents to spend their lunchtime or other free moments of the day with their children. This makes returning to work after maternity leave easier and provides some brief quality time with children for either parent.

3.   *Medical and Leave Benefits*

The federal government offers employees and their families an excellent selection of health benefit plans that continue coverage through retirement. In addition, in 1993, Congress passed the Family and Medical Leave Act (FMLA), which allows employees to take up to 12 weeks of unpaid leave, without fear of losing their jobs, to care for themselves while ill or care for a newborn, adopted child, or sick family member. In 1999, recognizing that many employees could not take the needed leave because they could not afford to go without pay for that time period, the President issued a memorandum allowing federal employees to use up to 12 weeks of accrued sick leave each year to care for family members suffering a serious health condition.

D.   The Disadvantages of Federal Employment

One of the most obvious disadvantages of working in the public sector is the salaries, particularly when compared to private practice. Large law firms in large cities pay top lawyers at least two or three times the salaries paid to comparable government positions. In-house corporate law departments and smaller or less urban law firms have salaries closer to government pay, but still generally higher. This is not an issue just for those who want to become rich. Many lawyers have school debts and/or family responsibilities that put pressure on them to bring home more income than a government salary provides.

There are other disadvantages related to the work environment. Many government legal offices do not have enough competent paralegal and clerical support. Fortunately, technology increasingly mitigates the impact of sparse clerical support. Government office spaces are generally smaller and less attractively furnished than those in the private sector, and lawyers are more likely to have to share space. Office equipment such as computers may not be the most up to date and may be in limited supply. Generally, government travel rules require that transportation and accommodation expenses conform to a very tight budget, even on long, difficult trips or extended assignments away from the office. And the government provides none of the special benefits found in the private sector, such as payment of bar association or club dues.

Unfortunately, the myth that government employees are incompetent or lazy may taint even the most professional and dedicated government lawyers. This can make it difficult to move into the private sector from a government job. Strict government ethics rules may limit mobility as well, at least for a certain time period. However, for many lawyers, such disadvantages do not outweigh the advantages of public-sector employment. In fact, the specialized and cutting-edge experience that public-sector international trade law lawyers acquire generally adds to their later marketability in the private sector.

E.   Opportunities in the Federal Government

The following federal government entities employ international trade lawyers:

Department of Commerce. The Department of Commerce is probably the largest single employer of international trade lawyers in the United States. Of the several hundred lawyers at Commerce, about 100 focus on international trade–related issues, including foreign market access and development, trade agreement compliance, foreign investment, export licensing, antidumping duties, countervailing duties, intellectual property rights, product standards, technology, telecommunications, environment, and fisheries. A comprehensive description of the Commerce legal offices can be located at www.ogc.doc.gov.

Office of the United States Trade Representative (USTR). USTR is part of the Executive Office of the President. Lawyers at

USTR provide advice on developing and coordinating U.S. international trade and investment policy, negotiating agreements with other countries on these matters, resolving disputes under these agreements, and handling related legislative initiatives. (See www.ustr.gov.)

Department of Agriculture. Agriculture has many overseas programs involving development of foreign markets for agricultural products and negotiation of international agricultural trade agreements. The department's international lawyers provide legal advice to Agriculture officials on all of these topics and work frequently with USTR. (See www.usda.gov.)

Department of State. The State Department's Office of Legal Advisor employs about 150 lawyers, who provide advice on international legal issues. Most work on public international law, including foreign policy and national security matters, but some State Department lawyers specialize in trade and private international law and work frequently with Commerce and USTR. (See www.state.gov.)

United States Agency for International Development (USAID). USAID lawyers provide advice on foreign assistance and humanitarian aid programs. (See www.usaid.gov.)

Department of the Treasury. Lawyers at the Treasury Department provide legal advice on matters relating to international financial/monetary affairs, including international debt and taxation matters, as well as trade and investment issues. (See www.treas.gov.)

Department of Homeland Security. Lawyers at U.S. Customs and Border Protection (formerly part of the Treasury Department) specialize in tariffs, quotas, and related issues. (See www.cbp.gov.)

Overseas Private Investment Corporation (OPIC). OPIC lawyers work on programs that provide loans, loan guarantees, and political risk insurance for investment projects in developing and transitional economies. (See www.opic.gov.)

Export-Import Bank of the United States (EXIM). EXIM lawyers advise on programs providing loans, loan guarantees, and export credit insurance to promote U.S. exports. (See www.exim.gov.)

The U.S. International Trade Commission (ITC). ITC lawyers support their agency's work as an independent, quasi-judicial federal agency that provides analytical trade expertise to both the legislative and executive branches of government, determines the impact of imports on U.S. industries, and directs actions against certain unfair trade practices, such as patent, trademark, and copyright infringement. (See www.usitc.gov.)

Many other federal departments and independent agencies hire lawyers who work on international aspects of their programs, including international trade or investment matters. A sample of these opportunities are listed as follows:

Department of Justice. The Justice Department has several offices employing international lawyers with such varying specialties as immigration law, foreign claims settlement, antitrust law, and other domestic criminal laws and federal programs with international implications. (See www.usdoj.gov.)

Environmental Protection Agency (EPA). The International Environmental Law Office in the EPA's Office of General Counsel provides legal services in connection with the international aspects of the EPA's environmental programs and also participates in the negotiation of international trade and investment agreements to ensure that environmental concerns are taken into account. (See www.epa.gov.)

Department of Labor. Certain international initiatives at the Department of Labor require legal advice. Labor lawyers often participate in negotiating international trade and investment agreements, particularly when immigration and worker rights are at issue. (See www.dol.gov.)

Food and Drug Administration (FDA). FDA lawyers engage in international activities, including the preparation of international agreements on product standards and scientific studies. (See www.fda.gov.)

F.   Conclusion

The opportunities described are only superficial summaries of the important work that awaits someone who practices international trade law in the public sector. When this work is joined with the balanced lifestyle generally possible in government employment, it makes for an exciting combination that should be considered by every young lawyer or law student who is interested in international law.

The Journey of a Private Practitioner Who Became an International Rule of Law Attorney

by Mary Noel Pepys

14

A. The Journey Begins

Fifteen years after graduating from law school, and having served as a government attorney in Washington, D.C. and a private practitioner in San Francisco, I decided in 1993 to embark on an unknown venture with the idealistic fervor of a Peace Corps volunteer. Despite my established professional life, lucrative income, and being in my forties, I volunteered for the newly created ABA Central European and Eurasian Law Initiative (CEELI) program, a technical legal assistance provider, created in 1990 by the ABA Section of International Law.

As the Berlin Wall was being dismantled, signifying the demise of communism, CEELI was created to support the efforts of former communist countries to build their democracies and market-based economies. These countries were faced with the daunting task of creating new legal systems, drafting new constitutions for their recently obtained independence, and writing a myriad of laws that embraced democratic principles and private commerce. The ABA believed that, by sending experienced American attorneys to serve as liaisons to live and work pro bono in Central and Eastern Europe and the former Soviet Union for an extended period of time, significant U.S. legal assistance could be provided to enhance the judiciary, legal profession, and legal education in all of these countries.

I volunteered with CEELI because I wanted to participate in the birthing process of democracy. I was intrigued by the prospect of working with lawyers and judges who lived under a political system that preached the supremacy of the State, and seemingly overnight changed its sermon to extol the virtues of democracy and of genuine public participation in government. I was curious how millions of citizens accustomed to State guarantees of housing, food, employment, medical care, even vacations, could suddenly assume the burdens of freedom, taking responsibility for their own lives.

After months of preparation and temporarily closing my office as a sole practitioner, I arrived in Sofia, Bulgaria, filled with hopes and expectations, but all I saw were grey skies, dull and dilapidated buildings, potholes large enough to sink trucks, and horrific emissions from buses and factories. Winter had set in, but the heating, which was central to the city, had not been turned on. The heat was turned on when the city bureaucrats decided to turn it on, and not a minute sooner. Once turned on, it was kept on 24 hours a day until spring. The only way I could regulate heat in my apartment was to open the windows—even during snowstorms. And I'm not getting paid for this? But I, like scores of other CEELI liaisons, did not join the program for the comforts of home. Otherwise, we would not have left. We joined as short-term volunteers to make a difference in the lives of others. Many of us continued with CEELI because our work to enhance the rule of law in former communist countries was fascinating. In the beginning, CEELI liaisons had to commit for at least six months, but many remained for a year or even two. I was a CEELI liaison for five years, living one year each in Bulgaria, Latvia, and Slovakia, and the remaining two years in Ukraine, Kazakhstan, and Croatia.

Following my five years of pro bono work with CEELI, I became a consultant to other rule of law technical assistance providers, which has given me the opportunity to work in such disparate countries as Mongolia, Papua New Guinea, Lebanon, Nepal, Algeria, and 30 other countries. But I am not alone. As I work around the world, I always find other former CEELI liaisons who have continued their rule of law work. Although we work in countries with vastly different political and legal systems, the nature of our work is similar, because the principles of judicial independence, legal profession, legal education, and human rights are international and transcend geographic borders.

B. The Substantive Work of International Rule of Law Attorneys

Imagine having your first meeting of the day with the Chief Justice of the Supreme Court. With the assistance of a translator, you discuss ways in which the governance structure of the judicial branch can be enhanced to ensure the independence of the courts. Transitioning from a history of subservience to the State, judges need not only to develop a structure that guarantees their independence, but also to learn how to assert their judicial prerogative. The meeting ends, and you, along with your translator, walk to the national bar association office, where a group of young lawyers is interested in creating a committee focused on strengthening their legal skills.

Because private practice is a relatively new concept in many former communist countries, these young lawyers want to learn best practices from experienced lawyers around the world. They ask many questions and are eager to learn from your expertise. You agree to meet again before heading off to your last meeting. The legal affairs committee of Parliament wants to draft a new law on legal education. Now that privatization is becoming an economic reality, the curriculum at law schools must be revised to incorporate the new laws pertaining to private property and a market-based economy. The parliamentarians with whom you meet are interested in obtaining curricula from a variety of American law schools. This is a typical day in the life of an international rule of law attorney.

The work as an international rule of law attorney is varied and includes writing constitutions, drafting laws incorporating democratic standards and market-based economic principles, and developing self-sustaining legal and judicial institutions. Essentially, the work ensures that the basic principles of protection of the human rights of citizens, equal treatment of all individuals before the law, and a predictable legal system with fair, transparent, and effective judicial institutions are pursued. Protecting citizens against the arbitrary use of state authority in countries with weak or newly emerging democratic traditions, where laws are neither fair nor fairly applied, and where judicial independence is compromised, is the foremost objective of international rule of law attorneys.

Areas in which international rule of law attorneys practice are:

- *Judicial Reform.* Increasing the independence of the judiciary by improving the administration of the courts and enhancing the competency, impartiality, and integrity of judges. In a democracy based on the rule of law, every citizen is entitled to a fair and timely hearing by an independent and impartial judicial tribunal conducted according to the due process of law. However, in many developing countries, judges are neither impartial nor committed to applying the law justly as they are dependent on political or other external factors, often because their appointment was based on their ideology rather than their competency. Because an independent judiciary is the cornerstone of a democracy based on the rule of law, this focal area is one of the highest priorities of rule of law assistance.

- *Legal Profession Reform.* Increasing the competency of the legal profession by developing voluntary bar associations to improve the education and ethics of attorneys, thereby enhancing their skills to serve as advocates for and protectors of the rule of law.

- *Legal Education Reform.* Assisting law schools to overhaul their curricula by integrating substantive courses based on new laws; incorporating practice-based legal education programs, such as moot court competitions, externship programs, pro bono clinics, and advocacy skills courses; and improving the skills of law professors by training them on modern adult-teaching techniques.

- *Criminal Law Reform.* Drafting and implementing modern criminal justice legislation to more effectively combat crimes, such as money laundering and cybercrime, and training criminal justice professionals, including prosecutors, investigators, and defense attorneys.

- *Human Rights and Postconflict Mitigation.* Increasing awareness of international human rights standards and humanitarian law, documenting human rights abuses, and training legal professionals to seek redress in the courts.

- *Anticorruption and Public Integrity.* Combating corruption and increasing transparency and accountability by developing national anticorruption action plans; drafting legislation on relevant issues, including freedom of information; implementing public integrity standards, and educating the public about the corrosive impact of corruption on society and the economy.

- *Gender Issues.* Educating governmental officials concerning the importance of women's rights issues, and assisting the government and nongovernmental organizations to address domestic violence, human trafficking, and sexual harassment in the workplace.

- *Institution Building.* Creating and supporting the organizational development and sustainability of indigenous institutions, which actively promote democratic reforms.

C. The Diplomatic Work of International Rule of Law Attorneys

In addition to knowing the substantive areas of rule of law assistance, international rule of law attorneys must be cognizant of and responsive to the needs and priorities of the local institutions in the countries where they work. Rather than insist on implementing the norms of developed countries, particularly the United States, attorneys must employ a consultative approach in providing technical assistance by working closely with local experts. Given that many of the countries where rule of law assistance is provided operate under a civil law system, the advice and technical assistance given by attorneys must be relevant to the unique problems of a civil law system. The U.S. legal system is only discussed when comparative models are requested, or, in some cases, where facets of the common law system (e.g., adversarial proceedings or jury trials) may be used as a model in judicial reform. In order to be truly successful, however, rule of law attorneys must be sensitive to and properly address the culture and customs of the country and individual practices.

D. Rule of Law Technical Legal Assistant Providers

The following providers and programs offer rule of law technical legal assistance:

1. The ABA Rule of Law Initiative

As a result of the success of CEELI, the ABA subsequently created four additional technical assistance programs for the other geographic regions: Asia, Africa, Latin America and the Caribbean, and the Middle East and North Africa. Today, the five regional rule of law technical assistance programs have been consolidated into a single entity called the ABA Rule of Law Initiative (ROLI). ROLI operates in more than 40 countries with a professional staff and a cadre of American volunteers: attorneys, judges, prosecutors, and law professors.

The mission of the ROLI is to promote the rule of law as one of the most effective long-term antidotes to the most pressing problems facing the world community today, including poverty, economic stagnation, and conflict. In promoting legal reform efforts, supporters of ROLI believe that addressing the global rule of law deficit, whereby people lack basic justice and economic opportunities, is an important mission of the international legal community.

2. United States Agency for International Development (USAID)

The major funder for rule of law technical assistance is the U.S. Agency for International Development (USAID), the principal U.S. federal government agency that provides assistance to countries engaging in democratic reforms and conflict prevention. USAID's efforts to enhance the rule of law are focused on three priority areas: supporting legal reform, improving the administration of justice, and increasing citizens' access to justice.

USAID rule of law technical assistance is carried out primarily through government contracts (although the ABA through ROLI primarily receives its USAID funding through grants) with a variety of for-profit companies and nonprofit organizations. Such firms include:

- AMEX International, Inc.
- Asia Foundation
- Associates in Rural Development, Inc. (ARD)
- Carana Corporation
- Casals and Associates, Inc.
- Checchi and Company, Consulting
- Chemonics International Inc.
- Creative Associates International
- DPK Consulting
- Democracy International, Inc.
- Development Alternatives, Inc.
- Development Associates, Inc.
- East West Management Institute
- Financial Markets International, Inc.
- International Foundation for Election Systems (IFES)
- Management Sciences for Development, Inc.
- Management Systems International
- Millennium/IP3 Partners, LLC

- National Center for State Courts
- PACT, Inc.
- PADCO
- Planning and Development Collaborative International
- Research Triangle Institute
- Urban Institute

3.   The World Bank

The World Bank is a vital source of financial and technical assistance to developing countries around the world and is made up of two development institutions: the International Bank for Reconstruction and Development (IBRD) and the International Development Association (IDA). Considerable rule of law work is conducted by the Justice Reform Practice Group of The World Bank.

4.   The Asia Development Bank, Inter-American Development Bank, and the African Development Bank

The Asia Development Bank, Inter-American Development Bank, and the African Development Bank are multilateral development finance institutions that promote, through loans and grants, democratic reform, economic and social development, and modernization of the state.

5.   The United Nations Development Programme (UNDP)

UNDP is the U.N.'s global development organization advocating change and providing solutions to those who confront national development challenges. One of the UNDP's major areas of focus is democratic governance. The UNDP International Legal Assistance Resource Center (ILRC), created by the ABA Section of International Law in December 1999, provides a legal resource capability to serve UNDP global governance programs and projects supporting legal reform and democratic institution building. The primary task of the ILRC is to assist UNDP country offices to identify candidates capable of providing legal advice, normally on a pro bono basis, on the drafting of legislation, judicial reform, building of legal institutions including professional groups and associations, and other legal dimensions of governance.

The ILRC-identified legal experts support UNDP in a wide array of substantive legal areas, including:

- Reform of legal institutions and systems, including reform of constitutional frameworks
- Support to electoral bodies and drafting of electoral laws
- Improvement of legislative drafting and parliamentary practices
- Reform of public-sector regulations and processes
- Strengthening anticorruption measures
- Support for decentralization and strengthening of local institutions
- Development of the capacity of independent lawyers associations
- Legal education and judicial training
- Legal services to the indigent and underrepresented

E. How to Become an International Rule of Law Attorney

One of the most effective methods for entering the increasingly competitive arena of international rule of law work, particularly for new attorneys who have little international work experience, is to obtain a volunteer position with the ABA Rule of Law Initiative.

To qualify as a volunteer, an attorney must have a minimum of five years of relevant experience, relevant substantive legal expertise, strong interpersonal skills, and a high level of energy and initiative. Although international experience and foreign language skills are not required, they give an applicant a competitive advantage. Thus emphasizing international experience, even if it is only personal travel, is advisable, as well as languages studied, even if not spoken fluently. Having worked abroad within the rule of law arena for a year or two, the opportunities for experienced rule of law attorneys are boundless.

F. Conclusion

International rule of law attorneys are in the enviable position of not only enhancing the capacity of local legal professionals, but also having a lasting impact on governmental and nongovernmental institutions involved in legal education, legal professional services, and judicial reform. Although the income of rule of law attorneys will not match that of private practitioners, the work of rule of law attorneys is priceless; it is exceptionally exciting, challenging, and supremely satisfying.[1]

---

[1] The International Development Law Organization has recently launched its online Rule of Law Directory at http://www.idlo.int/english/ ROLpage-ext/ROLHOME.asp. This is the first publicly available global inventory of rule of law assistance programs, and no password or subscription is needed.

Part 4

Practice Tips and Methodology

Using the Internet to Develop a Small-Firm International Law Practice

15

by Jeffrey M. Aresty and Edward Rholl[1]

A. Introduction

As emerging technologies become more important in defining new ways of practicing law over the Internet, the legal professional will be affected in a myriad of ways:

[1] The authors are working together to build the world's first virtual bar association, InternetBar.org, and its associated organization, IBO Institute, empowering a new breed of lawyers to practice, compete, and contribute to a globally connected society. The authors appreciate and acknowledge the contribution of Andrew Breines, Jeff Aresty's former law partner, who was the co-author of a prior version of this chapter. We also appreciate the wonderful editing skills of our colleague, friend, and editor, Salli Swartz.

- Bright young law students will have more chances than ever before to pursue careers in small-firm settings practicing private international law.
- Practicing lawyers everywhere can reinvent their practices in cyberspace and deliver legal information and services through the Internet in a wide variety of methods.
- There will be a need for lawyers to counsel and resolve disputes online.

Global cyber law is likely to become the most important field of legal study in the next decade. As the legal profession reinvents itself online, new roles for lawyers will also emerge. With the new information communications potential in the years ahead, this path may be the way for many law students who choose to pursue an international law career.

B. Working in a Global Legal Environment

1. The Impact of the Internet on the Practice of Law

The Internet is rapidly changing the way legal services must be delivered in order to match client demands. Much that was once billable must now be provided free of charge or for vastly reduced rates, because redundant or commodity-based legal work simply cannot command the high prices it once could.

For the small-firm lawyer, this is good news because it levels the playing field as more clients recognize that basic legal work is primarily created from forms and templates that are relatively equal in quality across any competent law firm. The world's largest global companies will continue to primarily engage the world's largest global law firms, but thousands, perhaps hundreds of thousands, of business clients increasingly value lower-cost service, technological acumen, and efficiency greater than they do the lush office interiors and high price tags of the mega-firms.

Most significantly, the Internet is rapidly changing the relative position of power between the legal profession and the clients it serves, particularly in the field of commercial and business law.

The Internet has spawned thousands of Web sites that provide legal information, legal-oriented products, and quasi-legal advice in a wide range of areas related to business and commercial law. People want to be empowered. They want answers quickly. They want to take responsibility, be proactive, and do some of their legal work themselves.

What has changed since this chapter was written for this book's second edition is the speed, quality, and breadth of information communications technologies (ICTs) that are now reaching even the smallest businesses in developing countries. Law students and young lawyers today will play a disproportionately important role and will become legal experts in the complex field of global cyber law, which is a daunting new area of the law.

2.   The Complexity of Cyber Law

Cyber law is complicated and complex: A photographer in Kansas can post her pictures to Shutter Stock (www.shutterstock.com) and sell them to a company in Hong Kong. What law will govern the sale? A jeweler in Egypt can sell his products via online catalogs at Blue Nile (www.bluenile.com). If a dispute arises, what jurisdiction will be competent? A coffee plantation in Kenya ventures with Starbucks and sells coffee in thousands of stores globally, as well as online from the Starbucks Web site. What governing law and jurisdictions will apply? Who will make these decisions? What lawyers and institutions will be involved?

3.   New Online Services

The emerging fields of online mediation and arbitration are radically changing the landscape of international dispute resolution. In the United Kingdom and Europe, companies like The Claim Room (www.themediationroom.com) and Juripax (www.juripax.com) are providing the online forum for companies throughout Europe to more quickly, efficiently, and directly resolve a wide range of disputes. In the United States, the vast commercial success of eBay is in no small measure due to its use of online dispute resolution tools created by Square Trade (www.squaretrade.com) that engender trust, reduce time and cost issues, and limit liability for the sellers. In addition, local courts are beginning to explore the use of Internet-based dispute resolution technology for small claims, family law, and other types of cases.

In the United Kingdom, nearly all personal injury cases must now go to mediation before any hearing in court. Money claims cases for UK plaintiffs and defendants can be made electronically, without a lawyer, using the Money Claim Online (MCOL) Internet service, provided by the government (https://www.moneyclaim .gov.uk/.

Another example is the joint venture between the American Arbitration Association and Cybersettle. Cybersettle's blind-bidding software, used as part of an online settlement process, is linked with American Arbitration Association conciliation, mediation, and arbitration.

What is truly exciting for the small-firm lawyer who is interested in an international practice is that the trend toward mediation and arbitration is now met by and even pushed by the emergence of these online spaces for case resolution. Because the greatest economies of usage fall into the realm of disputes between parties separated by hundreds or thousands of miles, the technology's promise is the greatest in the international realm. The small-firm lawyer with international interest and skill in using online mediation and arbitration will be increasingly in demand as counsel, advisor, or neutral.

4. The New Tools of Cyber Lawyers

During the last decade, a large cottage industry has sprung up, mostly online, which provides a stunning array of legal material at pennies on the dollar of what it would cost to get it from a law firm. Savvy lawyers welcome this change as a huge opportunity to expand their practices well beyond the traditional billable hour or contingency fee agreement. The most innovative firms offer free legal information online, the ability to schedule a telephone consultation online, and a secure extranet/Web space in which their clients may communicate and collaborate.

Lawyers who understand and master ICT and software applications that allow them to repurpose intellectual assets as legal information products will increase market position by providing deeply needed services to large numbers of people who are currently priced out of the market. At the same time, such lawyers will increase their business clientele and the scope of work done for that clientele by adapting the way they deliver services to the demands for efficiency and lower pricing coming from all corners of the business world.

For the small-firm international practitioner, there are several fun, engaging, and inexpensive ways to leverage technology and their own intellectual assets to create a mobile, client-centric, 24/7 law practice tailored for the networked world. First, lawyers can repurpose written materials as e-books, e-guides, and e-kits that can be sold as legal information products. Second, lawyers can create online education simply and inexpensively using tools like Power-Point and Articulate, and then publish these courses on their own Web sites as educational products. Lawyers can use blogs and pod-casts to communicate ideas, build brand awareness, and generate business. They can also publish podcasts, educational programs, and materials in the e-book genre on other Web sites catering to people seeking legal information. These legal information products can be provided free to generate client-based business, for a fee to generate non-billable hour revenue, or in both formats for different audiences. The provision of strictly legal information products, within the bounds of ethics and good judgment, will open a window to the global marketplace, establish you as a high-quality, trusted source of useful information, and almost inevitably lead to more traditional client business.

Moreover, as more relationships are moving online, trusted communities of lawyers (www.internetbar.org) are forming to shape a fair and accessible online justice system to meet society's needs. Finally, law firms can use tools such as virtual collaboration to expand their Web presence beyond simple online brochures to an interactive presence that has the power to change their practices.

C.   How We Use the Internet Effectively with Foreign Clients

Our firm provides international business law services to clients located outside the United States. One client located us on the

Internet through an international listing of business professionals. A colleague introduced the other client.

For the first client, we outlined the scope of services required via e-mail and telephone communications before entering into a fee agreement. Because the client is based in Canada and we are located in Boston, the Internet provided the best communications tool for this relationship. Because this Canadian client's service will be offered over the Internet to users around the world, there were several international legal issues, in addition to U.S. laws that had to be reviewed. International treaties (intellectual property and arbitration) were examined. U.S. and Canadian securities laws were examined and reviewed, in addition to specific communication with regulators in both countries. Because the client's business was somewhat novel, we were required to interpret existing law, policy, and culture in order to provide an opinion on how the regulators from different parts of the world would react. In the absence of a global rule, we had to help our client develop a globally compliant operational plan. We are exploring new technologies such as online deal rooms and online case management centers and examining how these online rooms will permit us to ameliorate the services we provide to our clients. Giving clients secure online access to their files and the firm research materials, along with the chance to communicate with us confidentially, will become the norm in the near future. These tools will replace the inconveniences of the time and cost of telephone calls and meetings with more efficient service and information.

A second client from the United Kingdom, referred to us via an e-mail from a colleague, had been selling its products in North America without a formal agreement for several years. We had an initial brief phone conversation at the outset of the relationship. From that point forward, the only communications were via e-mail and secure online meeting space. The client explained its initial needs, which were to draft a distribution and consignment relationship, and we provided a solution. We placed the draft of the document for review in a secure online space, where our comments were made asynchronously (saving on phone bills and sleep). The client wanted its existing relationships with its authorized agents in North America to remain unchanged. Because these relationships were not typical, the final agreements had to be specific to this relationship, and rules in both the United States and the United Kingdom had to be addressed. Because the laws and customs of the United Kingdom are not always similar to those in the United States, we retained UK counsel to provide an opinion regarding UK law. We established a virtual collaboration among ourselves, UK counsel, and the client.

D. Our Advice on Career Preparation

A traditional career in international law usually began in a large law firm in a cosmopolitan city, or in a job with the U.S. government in a trade or diplomatic role, or as legal counsel to a large multinational corporation. However, in recent years many types of small international business law firms have opened up, especially online, and provide a new career opportunity. It is much easier to establish a worldwide network of professional service providers and contacts by becoming active in international associations, such as the Section of International Law of the ABA (www.abanet.org/int), for example, and joining specialized groups of lawyers organized globally.

What type of personality is right for a small, private international law practice? Perhaps the most important quality is the ability to be a self-starter who can work independently with proper guidance and mentoring. Because you will be expected to handle many different matters in multiple jurisdictions during the course of each day, week, and month, your ability to properly segment each matter while prioritizing tasks is a valuable quality to cultivate and nurture. Some prioritizing will be dictated by the partners and senior associates at your firm. In some firms, experienced secretaries and paralegals who have long-standing relationships with small international law firms do the prioritizing and scheduling. Learning how to use the professional staff of your firm properly and effectively is another skill that can only be learned through experience.

There are certain skills to develop and tools to acquire that a young lawyer will need to be successful in this type of practice, detailed as follows.

1. The Tools

You will need to become familiar with the following tools:

1. Tools that will assist you to add efficiency, reduce redundant activity, and vastly reduce ethics and malpractice issues through rules-based online calendaring and communications functions

2. Work spaces including deal rooms, mediation and arbitration suites, online conferencing tools, e-learning suites, and client intranets and extranets

3. Communications tools including e-mail, blogs, podcasts, webcasts, global Internet telephony, Wikis, and instant messaging that help you practice constant communication with clients, prospects, and peers without being overwhelmed

4. Business development tools such as automated CRM, Web site templates, Really Simple Syndication (RSS), Web 2.0 social and business networking sites, and primary crossover with some of the tools listed above including blogs, podcasts, and e-learning suites

2. The Skills

You will want to develop the following skills:

- *Learn about the world's cultures.* Our firm hosts law clerk interns referred by Boston-area international language schools for one-month to one-year positions. These schools provide certificate and training programs to students from other nations and cultures who want to learn English. Many of these students have prior legal backgrounds or have complete law school in their home countries and are seeking practical experience with English in a professional setting. In addition to our international law clerks, we have one lawyer who is of counsel and has special skills in international law and international business consulting. We participate in and organize programs for international chambers of commerce on topics of international business law and meet people from other cultures who have moved to Boston. We attend programs at law schools with an international focus, and we have created a bar association on the Internet to connect people from every culture with each other in an effort to build trusted online communities to support the United Nation's Millennium Goals.

- *Acquire a strong and solid knowledge of many different legal areas.* Electronic commerce and the different laws that apply in different legal jurisdictions, privacy laws, global cyber law, U.S. securities and banking laws, tax laws, corporate laws, and intellectual property laws are all essential. It is useful to be fluent in many legal topics that can have an impact on international business. An excellent way to do that is to purchase a copy of the ABA *International Lawyer's Deskbook*, which provides a good overview of the many issues that require consideration before performing services for an international client.

- *Develop interpersonal skills to help you demonstrate that you understand your clients' legal concerns and that you can resolve them.* Many of the issues involved in international transactions contain cultural and communication obstacles that a simple document cannot overcome. Clients appreciate personal attention from lawyers, and a young lawyer who is properly prepared on a file is a second lawyer the client can hear from regularly. Learning how to communicate effectively with clients comes only from experience, and on-the-job training is the best way to learn. In fact, client contact in a small-firm setting can be a key to your personal growth as a lawyer. Clients come in all types and from all cultures in an international practice. Learning how to respond to each client will only add value to your legal career as you continue to learn and effectively manage your time and resources to the benefit of your clients. Only by demonstrating your understanding of how your client and its counterpart will form a lasting relationship can you fully and completely become an international business lawyer.

E.   Conclusion

Our experience of the changing nature of the legal practice and how lawyers will deliver services in the future serves to strengthen our belief that verbal and written communication, the ability to understand a client's business, and the ability to harness technology tools to deliver legal information and services to clients in the fast, efficient, and responsive way they now demand are the key ingredients to succeeding as an international business lawyer in the 21st century. Only by embracing technology and the transformation of the way that legal services are beginning to be delivered globally can you succeed in a small or midsize international business law firm.

Network or Not Work: The Choice Is Yours

16

by Mark E. Wojcik

A. Introduction

This book has laid out a wealth of practical information for those who are serious about making a career in international law. This chapter will remind you of points you found in earlier chapters, provide a few additional tips, and hopefully encourage you to develop short-term and long-range plans of action for your personal career success.

But first, a little background. For more than 15 years, I have taught international law and related international subjects, including international business transactions, international trade law, international human rights, and international criminal law. I have taught mainly at The John Marshall Law School in Chicago, but I have also been able to teach at law schools in Switzerland and Mexico, and in many other places around the world. I previously worked for a state government (when I clerked for a judge on the Nebraska Supreme Court), the U.S. government (when I clerked for a judge on the U.S. Court of

International Trade), and a foreign government (when I worked as Court Counsel to the Supreme Court of Palau, in western Micronesia). I have worked in private practice at a firm that specializes in customs and international trade law. And I am very active in the ABA Section of International Law and in other bar associations that focus on international law. My personal career path has been tremendously rewarding for me, and I hope to provide you now with some practical career advice that will help you either in getting started on your international job search or in focusing your present efforts into a more effective strategy.[1]

B.   A Five-Point Checklist

You may have already created a list of things to do from earlier chapters in this book. (If you haven't, take a moment now to look again at the parts you underlined or highlighted.) The list here of five suggestions is by no means an exhaustive list, and it should not replace your own personal to-do list that you created from other chapters of this book. But as you read, you will likely remember things that you should be doing to help your job search. The five points here may help you focus on an action plan that you need to put into place now.

1.   Look at Your Résumé with the Eyes of an Employer

If you have not yet written a résumé, make that your first task. If you need help doing this, consult a legal résumé writing guide. If you have a résumé that you have used in a country other than the United States and if you are looking for a job here, you should know that American résumés might be quite different from ones that are common in other countries. Conversely, if you are seeking a job in another country, you should at least know what information is commonly contained on résumés in that other country. Get a résumé

---

[1] If you would like to know more about my personal background and career path, see Mark E. Wojcik, *Practical Career Advice for Young International Attorneys: How to Build a Killer Resume, Network Effectively, Create Your Own Opportunities, and Live Happily Ever After*, 5 ILSA J. Int'l & Comp. L. 455 (1999).

guide with samples that will give you ideas and suggestions on changes that you might have to make. You can buy a résumé guide in a bookstore or online, or if you are near a law school (or maybe even still in law school), you can see what resources are available in the career service office.

If you already have a résumé, be sure it is up to date. Keep it current with your employment history, education, bar association memberships, publications, and presentations. I advise keeping a basic résumé that includes all of your information, even if it means that your résumé is several pages long. When you apply for a particular job, you can go to that current résumé, remove information that might not be relevant for a particular job, and focus it to the specific job you are seeking. Such is the wonder of résumés on computer—it is no longer necessary to have a one-size-fits-all résumé. You can focus your résumé to make you a better match for each particular job opportunity.

Once your résumé is finished (or nearly so), make an appointment with the Career Service Office if you are still in law school and ask them to meet with you to discuss the strengths and weaknesses of your résumé. Before you meet with the Career Service Office, you should drop off a copy of your résumé in advance so that the comments you receive are more meaningful. The services of your school's Career Service Office will still be available to you even if you have already graduated, so do not be shy about using them. If you no longer live near your alma mater, call them anyway and arrange for a telephone consultation to discuss your résumé (you may also e-mail or fax your résumé to them for comments). Also ask them about reciprocal career service arrangements that your school may have with the career service offices of other schools near where you currently live.

When you meet with the Career Service Office, be as specific as you can about your dream job. If a listing for that job comes in later that afternoon, the persons you told will know to call you first, even before they post the job for others to see. Hopefully you will receive useful advice from having the Career Service Office look at your résumé, but no two individuals will have the same experience. Many career service offices have little direct experience in helping people find international jobs. They may be confused about what the term means and may think that you are looking only for a job in another country. They may tell you (wrongly) that international law can only be practiced in a large city such as Washington, D.C. or New York. You should still meet with the career office, however, because you are seeking basic advice on your résumé, to be sure that it is in the best shape possible—and they can certainly help you with that. Hopefully they will help guide you along other parts of your career search as well, but you may have to educate them about the wide range of international law careers.[2]

After you meet with the professionals in the Career Service Office, repeat the exercise with trusted friends and colleagues who are working in law firms or other jobs. Ask them simply to look at your résumé to be sure that it is in the best shape possible. You will often be amazed at how helpful this can be.

The persons looking at your résumé will help you proofread it (although you should always do your own proofreading as well). I cannot tell you how many times I find typos in a résumé—even, for example, in the person's e-mail address. (How can you expect to get a job offer if the e-mail address on your résumé is wrong?) But persons who look at your résumé are more than a proofreading service, and you should ask them to look at your résumé the way that an employer would. Have them be critical and seek out specific comments on anything you should change in the résumé. For example, persons looking at your résumé may offer you some tips on how to make it more professional. You might be using a personal e-mail address that suggests you are not an ideal employee (e.g., partygirl@gmail.com might raise eyebrows). Persons looking at your résumé might point out that it is not as focused as you think it is. For example, if you are looking for a career involving some aspect of international law, there should be something on your résumé to indicate that interest. You might have forgotten to list that you are a member of the American Bar Association Section of International Law or a member of the international law committee of a state or local bar association.

---

[2] You may, for example, want to buy them a copy of this book as a present.

When you send your résumé to other people, you are also actively enlisting their help in your job search. They will keep an eye out for opportunities that might be right for you.

2. Join Professional Associations

If your résumé is not as strong as you would like it to be, see what you can do to build it up quickly. If you are a student, be sure that you are a member of the International Law Society at your school. I'm amazed at how many students seeking international careers will not even take this simple step. The dues are usually nominal, if there are any at all.

At some law schools, the International Law Society may be dormant, which sometimes happens after the president and other officers graduate without electing successors. Find out what you need to do to start it up again. Congratulations, you have not just become a member, but you have likely also become the new President of the International Law Society. This advice holds true for any student organization. If you are interested in international child abduction, you should join the Children's Law Society. If you are interested in international issues affecting the environment, you should join the Environmental Law Society. If no society exists directly affecting your interests, you should start a new one. For example, if you are interested in international criminal law, you can create a new International Criminal Law Society.

You should join bar associations—not only the American Bar Association and its Section of International Law, but also state and local bar associations that may have international committees. (If you are a law student, remember that you can join bar associations as a student member.) Bar associations provide excellent opportunities to network. Be sure to join not only the associations, but also the specific committees that are of particular interest to you.[3] These committees are smaller groups, focused on your areas of interest. You may soon find that you will be asked to lead the group.

---

[3] In the unlikely event that there is no committee of interest to you, ask the bar association leaders how you can start a new committee. Again, you will instantly become the leader of that new group, and you may be able to use that leadership position in helping you to find a job.

If the bar association does have a committee of interest to you, then you should attend the next meeting and introduce yourself to the chair and vice-chair of the committee. Offer your assistance to them. They will greatly appreciate your offer and remember your name. You can offer to help organize a speaker for a future meeting, or, more ambitiously, offer to help organize a panel of speakers for a continuing legal education (CLE) program. You can offer to write or edit a newsletter for the committee. For some strange reason, no one else wants this job, even though it gives you an opportunity to promote your name and will give you visibility within the bar association committee. Be sure that the newsletter becomes a place where committee members will post job openings. When you are the editor of the newsletter, you also will be the first person to see that new job listing.

When you are working on programs, remember to identify topics that might be of interest to other committees or sections in the bar association. The criminal law committee, for example, may be interested in a program on recent developments in extradition. The family law committee may be interested in a program on international adoption or child kidnapping. Whatever topic you choose for a program, be sure to focus on recent developments in that area. Audience members are more likely to come if new information is discussed, rather than presenting things they can read about in hornbooks.

I have found my memberships in professional bar associations to be particularly rewarding, both in terms of the substantive opportunities I have been able to cultivate and the personal friendships I have made over the years. I have found that those who are most active in bar associations are often also the happiest lawyers I have met. They have found ways of balancing their professional and personal lives.

3. Invite Prospective Employers as Speakers

When you are the one organizing a panel or program for a student group or bar association committee, you can pick the speakers. Pick speakers who are working at the places where you want to work. Law students (and many lawyers) are often surprised at the generosity of attorneys and others who will agree to speak to their groups. Most will do it for free. (If they won't do it for free, ask someone else.) For the speakers, the invitation to speak is an opportunity to contribute as well as an opportunity to promote the law firm (or other entity where they are working).

If you don't know who to ask to be a speaker, ask a professor or a bar association leader to speak on a recent international development or to give suggestions for speakers. The Career Service Office, the Alumni Office, and the bar association will also have names of potential speakers. Ideally, you want to invite speakers from places where you want to work. If you want to work at the largest international law firm in town, invite a partner or senior associate from that firm to speak. Make the speaker feel important. Create a nice sign to announce the event, be sure the room is set up, and find an audience. One way to double a potential audience is to co-sponsor your event with other groups if possible. You instantly have twice the membership base for your speaker. Be the one to greet the speaker at the door, and be sure the speaker learns your name. Gush about your speaker's accomplishments during your introduction. Have a camera to take pictures of the speaker during the talk, and later with you. Send a thank-you letter after the event, and include a copy of the photograph if you both look good. Put your names on the back of the photo and jot down the date and place of the event. Give a copy of the photo to the student newspaper or bar association newsletter and ask them to run it. Send a copy of the paper to your speaker, who will enjoy the unexpected additional publicity. (Do not enclose a résumé, however; the time will come for that later.)

Here is the secret: If you want to work at a particular place, invite someone who works there now to be the speaker (either as a career talk or on some substantive aspect of the person's work). You will gain some valuable inside information about that job, how to prepare for it, and what it is really like once you get it.

4. Keep Current

If you hope to work in international law, you must be informed about current events. You may find yourself at a party or a seminar needing to say something meaningful about the state of the world. You should read a newspaper with good coverage of international issues. The *New York Times*, for example, might be a good choice, and it is easy to find in print or online. You should also read a newspaper or news magazine from outside the United States to give you differing perspectives on issues. Choices here might include the *Financial Times* of London or another source. Learn how to get these foreign news sources off the Internet, but be careful that your "surf" time is focused on news that will benefit your career search.

You cannot limit yourself to newspapers and the Internet. You must also tackle more complex readings on international developments. *Foreign Affairs* and *Foreign Policy* are two well-known journals that will give you the depth of analysis that you need to cultivate. International law journals are an obvious choice as well, including the Year-in-Review issue of *The International Lawyer* published by the ABA Section of International Law.

Keeping current with recent cases is also important, and you should make it a point to read advance sheets or subscribe to e-mail services that will link you to the most recent cases. For example, if you are interested in immigration law, you should be reading the immigration cases that come down across the country. If you are interested in customs and international trade, you should be reading the new decisions from the U.S. Court of International Trade and the trade cases from the U.S. Court of Appeals for the Federal Circuit. Keep up on legislative and administrative developments too. Keeping current will also help you identify topics and speakers for any programs you might be organizing.

5.   Write Something, and Before You Publish It, Ask an Expert to Read It

You need to have a writing sample, no matter what. You may as well have a writing sample that has been published somewhere. As you read articles from law journals and bar association magazines on a regular basis, you will realize that writing an article is also something that you can do. Pick a topic about which you already know something, or pick a topic about which you would like to learn something and write it up. Do not be afraid of making mistakes in what you write. Mistakes happen. Even the venerable *Black's Law Dictionary* (in an earlier edition) stated that "to be valid . . . treatises [sic] must be approved by two-thirds of the Senate." Wouldn't Williston and Prosser be surprised to learn that their books are not valid because they were never subjected to U.S. Senate confirmation? The definition should read "treaties," of course. In reviewing student papers, I often must read about violations "of the statue [sic]," and I wonder what piece of art has been vandalized. I read about the decision of the "trail court," and wonder if it meant deciding whether to camp for the night. You must proofread your drafts carefully to avoid these errors; do not rely solely on spell check or on the skills of your editors. While you may be able to survive these errors at a later stage of your career (say, for example, after you get tenure at a law school), you cannot afford to make such mistakes when you are building your reputation.

Beyond simple proofreading, however, is the need for serious substantive analysis of what you have written. You should not hesitate to send drafts of your articles to leading authorities in the field and to ask them to look at your work before it is published. If they agree, you will have the benefit of their expertise. Remember to thank them appropriately and to credit them for their assistance. After they have reviewed your article, you can also ask them to have a look at your résumé. Your résumé may be perfect by this point, but ask them for their advice about it anyway. If you haven't landed a job by now, there may be a way to recraft your résumé or to deliver it to an appropriate hiring partner or agency.

C. Getting to Work on Getting Work

The advice in this chapter—and in this book—should help you focus your search for an international career. Decide what steps you need to take now, in the next week, and in the next year. Stay involved and stay focused, and don't be afraid to ask others for help along the way.

Creative Strategies for Launching and Growing an International Law Practice

17

by Janet H. Moore

A. Introduction

Perhaps no other legal field is as vast—and as mesmerizing—as international law. Whether you pursue a career in international litigation or arbitration, international trade, cross-border business transactions, public international law, or another specialty, intellectual challenges await. As you climb the international law career ladder, refer to the following tips to propel your career forward.

B. Responding to Globalization

According to author Thomas Friedman, the world is flat—and getting flatter by the minute.[1] This means that to be successful in a global economy, lawyers must cultivate a global perspective, versatility, and cross-cultural competence. It also means that lawyers who embrace these trends will have an advantage over those who do not.

1. Take a Global View

Success as an international attorney requires not only great legal skills but also an understanding of global trends. Effective lawyers in a global economy stay abreast of trends in international business and other sectors, and figure out ways that these trends might impact their clients. A global outlook will help you anticipate and steer your clients clear of problems—problems that less internationally sophisticated attorneys would miss. Clients will appreciate your foresight.

2. Become Versatile

Although international lawyers often develop specialized niches during their careers, they also benefit from staying versatile. As globalization spreads, so will the demand for versatile lawyers who can handle a variety of issues with aplomb—even when finding clear answers across jurisdictions and legal systems becomes impossible.

David Morley, Worldwide Managing Partner of Allen & Overy, articulated the importance of this quality when he said, "[W]e need to develop versatile lawyers capable of working in more than one discipline. So when a partner has career discussions with an associate who wants to experience other practice areas, we must encourage that where we can."[2]

---

[1] Thomas Friedman, *The World is Flat: A Brief History of the 21st Century* (New York: Farrar, Straus and Giroux, 2006).

[2] "We listened to associates. Now partners have to do their bit," by David Morley, Allen & Overy, in Lawyer.com, October 23, 2006.

Lawyers can heighten their versatility by working on a variety of matters—not enough to become specialists in multiple fields, but enough to spot critical issues. Attorneys with general international practices and lawyers stationed in foreign offices (far from their home office specialists) particularly need such versatility.

3. Cultivate Cross-Cultural Competence

Effective lawyers communicate with their clients in a way that helps clients absorb the information that has been relayed. Whether your clients are businesspeople, law students, or government employees, having good people skills—and cross-cultural acumen—will improve your effectiveness.

International rainmaking also requires cross-cultural competence. As discussed later in this chapter, you will need powerful and plentiful personal connections, and strong, culturally appropriate communication skills to become a rainmaker. Many of the lawyers that I train in global rainmaking techniques feel somewhat anxious about the client development process. Finding a comfortable style and learning to build trust across cultures becomes vitally important to their international rainmaking success.

You can cultivate your cross-cultural competence by interacting regularly with people from other cultures, both in your professional and personal life. When you do so, enhance your rapport by matching the other person's pitch, pace, inflection, and body language. Before meeting a potential client or employer from another culture, research that culture's norms of social behavior. Helpful books about the social customs across the globe include Roger Axtell's *Gestures: The Do's and Taboos of Body Language around the World*. Employees of foreign embassies, foreign consulates, and the U.S. State Department's country-specific desks often will share their insights over the telephone. The Web sites of the U.S. State Department and Central Intelligence Agency also publicize important information about countries worldwide.

Most attorney-client communication now occurs via e-mail and other technology-based methods. This means that when you have the chance to spend time with a client in person, make that time count favorably. If you do not, dozens of culturally and client-savvy attorneys will be waiting in the wings to take your place.

C. Launching an International Law Career

Most law graduates at the top of their class at a stellar law school easily break into the international law field. However, lawyers without such credentials can also succeed if they: (1) persevere; (2) network constantly and strategically; (3) brand and market themselves appropriately; (4) cultivate and use excellent people skills; (5) produce impeccable work; and (6) willingly take zig-zag steps up the career ladder. The following steps will help you achieve these goals.

1. Clarify What You Seek

As an aspiring international lawyer, you should clarify which legal area you want to pursue—whether litigation, arbitration, transactional, trade, criminal, or any of the other international specialties. Understand and make sure that you are willing to tackle the accompanying complexities, uncertainties, and demands. Knowing which area interests you most will focus your career efforts.

Until you decide, investigate several areas simultaneously. Informational interviews, networking, and continuing legal education classes are good ways to find out about practice specialties and to narrow your job search. Consider charting the pros and cons of each specialty as you go along to evaluate your options. Once you have clarified your area of interest, define your ultimate dream job. Then set yearly, monthly, and perhaps weekly goals to move you forward. Formulate specific action steps as you gather more information, and have a peer, colleague, or lawyer coach hold you accountable for your progress.

As you select your international career path, keep in mind that clients now have access to less expensive but acceptable legal services. Outsourcing legal work to offshore attorneys will continue to grow in popularity. Make sure that your legal work is not so rote that it can be easily handled by offshore attorneys.

2. Conduct a Self-Assessment

Highly effective lawyers—regardless of their field—communicate clearly with others. Many of these lawyers also know how to create a favorable impression when they meet other people.

The first step to creating a good impression is to figure out how others perceive you. Assessments like DiSC™ and Meyers-Briggs™ will give you objective feedback about your strengths, weaknesses, personality type, and communication style. Draw on this data to improve your people skills and help you pick a practice area that complements your natural strengths. For example, if you are an extrovert, you would probably thrive in a heavy courtroom practice—but wither in an isolated, research-based position.

Sometimes there will be cultural barriers to your ideal career path. A former female colleague of mine was determined to represent American corporate clients in the Middle East; she succeeded, but finally found the cultural barriers too wearing. Many, but not all, limitations can be overcome with hard work. Understand your hurdles and honestly assess whether you can overcome them.

3.   Polish Interview Skills

As you prepare to interview, try to correct any nervous habits that you might have, like twitching or poor eye contact. Videotape yourself while giving a presentation or during a mock client interview; this can be an invaluable tool for recognizing unflattering personal habits. Honing your interview skills will also prepare you for public presentations and client interviews down the road. Videoconference interviews have become very common, especially when employers and job candidates are geographically distant. Because the camera magnifies nervous habits and shiny or overly decorative clothing, act and dress accordingly.

4.   Bolster Needed Experience

Some aspiring international lawyers need to bolster their international experience before they can break into the field. As you examine yours, think creatively about any international exposure you gained through nonlegal work, such as volunteer work or domestic projects with tangential international issues. This experience will boost your credibility. If you lack international experience, obtain some through pro bono, contract, or consulting work with cross-border issues. Many international nonprofit organizations, such as those involved in developing countries, regularly seek volunteers and short-term employees.

According to Dean Robert Gallucci of the Edmund A. Walsh School of Foreign Service of Georgetown University, it is important to get international experience "so that you start to underline for your later career moves an early interest in international affairs."[3] Nonlegal jobs that develop international business acumen will also strengthen your marketability, particularly for certain consulting and in-house legal positions.

5. Network Vigorously

Whether you are an experienced international practitioner or a foreign LL.M. student searching for your first job, regular and effective networking will galvanize your career success. While job hunting, contact distant connections as well as close ones. Contacting weak ties has been linked to job search success because these remote connections will know of job opportunities not familiar to your close friends and family.[4]

Make as many meaningful connections as you can with other lawyers in the field. Interacting regularly with experienced international lawyers will build your network of contacts and deepen your understanding of the practice area. You may even get helpful hints about choosing competent foreign counsel and other practical advice.

Mingle with international lawyers at the continuing legal education classes and meetings sponsored by the international sections of local bar associations, the American Bar Association, and the International Bar Association. Or, sample some of the programs offered by the many bar associations that focus on particular ethnic groups, such as the Hispanic National Bar Association.[5] Getting involved with such organizations will multiply your network of international contacts.

This kind of targeted networking can bring tremendous results. Not long ago, I coached an aspiring international lawyer

---

[3] Interview with Robert L. Gallucci, Dean of the Edmund A. Walsh School of Foreign Service at Georgetown University, January 31, 2007, available at www.InternationalLawyerCoach.com.

[4] Mark Granovetter, "The Strength of Weak Ties: A Network Theory Revisited," *Sociology Theory*, Vol. 1 (1983).

[5] The Hieros Gamos Web site (www.hg.org) lists many internationally focused bar associations.

who had international credentials but a purely domestic law practice. At a particular bar event, he connected with an experienced international practitioner who needed a law partner with my client's background. They decided to form a partnership virtually on the spot. Such instant chemistry may be unusual, but it illustrates how networking with experienced practitioners can benefit aspiring international lawyers.

6. *Research the Culture of Potential Employers*

Each place of employment has an internal culture. Try to learn as much as you can about this culture in advance by talking to former and current employees and reading information on the Internet. Make sure that you would feel comfortable working within the employer's culture.

One of my clients left his large international firm when he realized that its offices were too combative—and that the firm's culture not only tolerated but promoted this atmosphere. Another client found that her international trade organization rarely promoted employees from within, stifling her career climb. In both of these cases, advance research might have uncovered these problems.

Conversely, sometimes lawyers discover a potential employer with an ideal culture. One of my clients happily left her comfortable but staid job upon finding a multinational corporation that encouraged its attorneys' autonomy and creativity. A job that matches your values and lets you utilize your natural talents can bring real career satisfaction. Of course, you should also assess each prospective employer's plans for responding to globalization.

Studies show that people feel comfortable with others who are like themselves, so you want to fit in as much as possible during each interview. For example, if you are interviewing with an international high-tech company, casually mention some relevant industry terminology, which you can glean from trade publications. Or, if you are interviewing for a job with a particular legal specialty, become conversant in the fundamental concepts, jargon, and acronyms of that specialty. Try to use idioms common to the potential employer's parlance; for example, if you are an Argentine lawyer interviewing with a Mexican employer, incorporate some of the colloquialisms of Mexican Spanish. If you are not a native speaker of the language in which you are interviewing, polish your written and spoken language skills ahead of time with a tutor.

7. Seek International Work Wherever You Land—And Do It Well

Thanks to globalization, many domestic law jobs now include tangential international work. Constantly seek and ask your employer for projects with international aspects. For example, if you have a family law or probate practice, look for projects involving foreign parties or foreign assets. In litigation, take on cases involving issues of foreign law or evidence, with litigation experts or witnesses located abroad. Working on cross-border issues will build your international expertise, confidence, and contacts. Be sure to develop strong relationships with foreign counsel whenever possible; they may become good referral sources.

Of course, once you get a cross-border project, you should produce an excellent final product. Work hard and let your talent shine. Lawyers' reputations follow them throughout their careers, so do the best you can on every assignment—whether international or not.

8. Ask for What You Want

Whether you desire more international work, mentorship by a senior international lawyer, increased job responsibility, or business from a prospective client—ask for what you want. Do not expect others to read your mind. Be sure to request performance feedback from clients and employers throughout your career. Although momentarily painful, negative feedback will enable you to improve. Conversely, when you get positive feedback from a client or boss, ask for a letter of recommendation. Legal recruiters report that too many job candidates lack letters of recommendation, and have difficulty getting them after the fact.

D. Climbing the Career Ladder

Once you have launched your career, continue to look ahead. Whether you aspire to a promotion or a new job, keep your goals in mind.

1. Develop Portable Business

Nowadays, a lawyer's success and longevity at a law firm hinge on individual rainmaking (bringing in new business). Law firm practitioners, whether junior or senior, should take immediate steps to develop their pipeline of business, even if doing so does not come instinctively.

During one of my training programs in global rainmaking, a relatively new partner at a large international firm blurted out, "I hate talking to potential clients at parties, and I don't want to do any client development!" Like many lawyers, he was intimidated by client development and wanted to rely on his partners to supply his work. (Needless to say, his partners appeared unhappy at his revealing outburst.)

If you hesitate to develop clients, identify and grapple with your barriers to rainmaking. Even lawyers who struggle with introversion or shyness can devise client development strategies that feel comfortable; rainmaking may never be completely natural, but it does become easier with customized strategies.

One key to rainmaking success is to develop techniques suited to your individual strengths. For example, I worked with one introverted international lawyer who abhorred mingling at large gatherings. We worked on strategies for connecting with people one-on-one at those events, making them less intimidating. In another case, a very gregarious client needed to modify his networking style so that he made fewer—but more meaningful—connections. Yet another international attorney worked to implement a marketing plan from the ground up; as a recent partner, she found herself cast adrift without clients and without rainmaking experience. All of these attorneys found that by choosing rainmaking activities that matched their personal styles and maximized their individual strengths, they followed through with client development consistently and successfully.

Any client development effort should begin with an ideal client profile. Define your ideal clients, and then prepare a client development plan to reach them. Find other professionals—such as money managers and accountants—with the same ideal clients, and share referrals. For example, a U.S. immigration lawyer who wants to help professionals relocate from Asia could cultivate relationships with real estate agents who serve those clients.

Attend events that attract your ideal clients. For example, many trade groups (such as those in the energy industry) and internationally focused nonprofits, like chapters of the World Affairs Council, attract international executives to their educational lectures. Participating in these kinds of events will expose you to both potential clients and referral sources.

Lawyers who work globally know that a close personal relationship often must precede a substantial business relationship. For this reason, cultivating certain foreign clients will take longer than cultivating American ones. Before interacting with potential clients, polish your cross-cultural skills. Show an interest in your client's culture by learning some basic pleasantries in the client's native tongue. Many American lawyers' direct communication makes clients from other cultures uncomfortable. Moreover, these clients may be far too polite to mention the offense, but they may never call again. Personal introductions and recommendations matter a great deal in many cultures. Lawyers who aspire to international rainmaking should ask their contacts to make introductions on their behalf, and then follow up in a culturally sensitive manner.

Just as you would research the culture of a potential employer, research the culture of potential clients and their industries. Find out as much as possible about each individual with whom you will meet—their experience, schooling, interests, and the like. Figure out any natural connections between you that might create rapport. Customize your firm's marketing materials, and adapt your pitch to the client's unique needs and culture. Even governmental and in-house attorneys should cultivate their rainmaking savvy. This skill will be critical if they transition to private practice. Knowing how to satisfy clients certainly helps any lawyer succeed, whether in a government, nonprofit, law firm, in-house, or academic practice.

2. Brand Yourself

Your personal brand (or reputation) is what comes to mind when others think of you. If you do not know what your brand is, solicit input. E-mail 10 to 20 colleagues, peers, and clients and ask them to respond with 5 to 10 words or phrases that describe you.

Encourage both positive and negative feedback. You will probably find that many of the comments are similar, and these reflect the strongest part of your brand.

Through this exercise, one of my Type A clients unhappily discovered that others perceived her as tardy. In her zeal to please, she had taken to promising speedy turnarounds to her work—and then slightly missing her deadlines. Unfortunately, this tarnished her brand. She used the invaluable feedback to improve her timeliness and reputation.

You can also enhance your public image by consciously and authentically showcasing your expertise. According to Frank Sommerfield, President of Sommerfield Communications, Inc., "In a highly competitive professional services environment, people need to stand out not just based on the quality of their work and their commitment. People with the most influence—and in the most demand—are known also for their 'thought capital,' the novel expertise and perspective that makes others want them at the table. That's the basis of a strong 'personal brand.'"[6]

Look for ways to enhance your brand by demonstrating your knowledge. Some attorneys share their wisdom through newer technology like blogs[7] and podcasts. Others brand themselves as experts through traditional means, like writing articles or giving speeches and interviews and then posting them on a Web site. Although every attorney must carefully comply with applicable state bar rules, law firm brochures and other marketing materials can also promote international expertise.

As previously discussed, lawyers must pay attention to the impressions they create. Improve the impression that you make by introducing yourself in a clear way. This will reinforce your brand in the other person's mind. For example, instead of saying "I'm an international trade lawyer," you might say, "I'm a lawyer who helps companies overcome trade barriers so that they can

---

[6] E-mail to Janet H. Moore dated June 6, 2007.

[7] For example, Dan Harris of Harris & Moure, PLLC, has enhanced his brand as a China law expert through his China Law Blog (www.chinalaw blog.com.)

sell their products internationally." Try to paint a vivid and memorable picture of what you do.

3.   Connect Daily

Why network when you can connect instead? According to Keith Ferrazzi's *Never Eat Alone*, connecting means sharing knowledge and resources, time and energy, friends and associates, along with empathy and compassion in a continual effort to provide value to others, while coincidentally increasing your own personal value.[8] Try to make connections for others—to help them in some way— for the pleasure of it.

When you connect with someone, try to create quick rapport. You make an immediate connection by listening attentively and demonstrating interest and enthusiasm for what the other person is saying. Do it out of the sincere desire to connect with someone. If you have a hidden motive of getting something in return, you may alienate the other person.

4.   Seek Assistance

Whether you are at the beginning or tail end of your career, ask for professional help if you need it. A professional career counselor, lawyer coach, state bar, or alumni career center will have many resources to propel you forward. Legal recruiters can also provide invaluable help. Most have a good sense of the current job market and can tweak your résumé to increase your marketability.

You may need to make multiple career moves—some lateral and some upward—to reach your ultimate career goal. Long gone are the days when an international lawyer would make partner at a firm and stay there throughout his or her career. Many attorneys transition between the public and private sectors or jump between law firms and companies. Regardless, clarify your goals and values through self-assessments to ensure that any job change brings personal satisfaction.

---

[8] Keith Ferrazzi, *Never Eat Alone: and Other Secrets of Success, One Relationship at a Time* (New York: Doubleday, 2005), p. 8.

E. Conclusion

The world desperately needs more lawyers with international experience and interest. In return, lawyers joining this practice can look forward to years of intellectual challenge, endless variety, and deep satisfaction.

One Non-Linear Career in International Law

18

by Homer E. Moyer, Jr.

Being asked to reflect on one's own career may be flattering, but it is also a bit daunting. It brings to mind a worrying comment that a friend passed on to me not long ago: "some of the things I remember best never actually happened." Although I won't make that my disclaimer, I am nonetheless mindful that past successes are sometimes more readily recalled than frustrations, which we all encounter. Understanding that, I am happy to venture a few subjective observations-in-hindsight about an unplanned career in international law.

My career path should give heart to any lawyers who worry that they were not properly prepared for the paths on which they find themselves. A career in international law is something for which I was, in

virtually all respects, unprepared. Like most of my college classmates—and unlike all of my children—I never had a semester
abroad. Of the 30 classmates in my section of the law school
dorm, I quickly learned that I was the only one never to have
traveled abroad. At law school, I never took a course in international law. I had no foreign language skills, other than unhelpful
remnants of Spanish vocabulary.

Although I was plainly above average in international illiter-
acy, our profession at that time also had some way to go. The
international law courses offered in law school tended to be on
public international law only. There were no courses on international trade or the GATT, and those curious classmates who were
interested in a career in international law had relatively few job
opportunities. With one or two exceptions, there were no multinational law firms with offices in multiple countries. The State
Department's Legal Adviser's Office and one or two public financial institutions interviewed at our law school, and a few large
New York and Washington firms did exotic-sounding international
work. Otherwise, international law was not a well-trodden career
path. Rather, the common paths were those you might expect:
clerkships, large firms with strong corporate, litigation, or regulatory practices, and—as this was during the Vietnam War—many
opportunities for military service.

My own path led through Navy JAG (and its excellent, no-frills
litigation skills training, which was then a rarity in law schools),
an 18-month stint with a public interest organization that had an
interest in supporting a treatise/casebook on military law, and
three invaluable years at Covington & Burling, where that firm's
standards of excellence were forever inculcated in my professional DNA. All of those stops were in Washington, D.C., and were
thus landlocked (moderately embarrassing for a Naval officer)
and entirely domestic. Each was a wonderful experience, but none
pointed to a career in international law.

There was no foreseeing then that some day I might chair
the Section of International Law of the ABA, an entity that was
undoubtedly unknown to me at the time. My career swerve into
international law came when, thanks to my friend and classmate,
J.T. Smith, and his extraordinary mentor, Secretary Eliot Richard-

son, I was invited to join them at the Department of Commerce. I recall that the White House personnel office and I both initially balked at the idea, but J.T. and Eliot persevered. As a result, I had a uniquely rich government experience and, ultimately, a clear change of direction in my legal career.

One milestone came barely a year later when, following quick enactment of the Anti-Boycott law during the early months of the Carter Administration, a new Deputy Assistant Secretary and I were locked in a room for weeks and charged with producing implementing regulations. Out of that crucible came perhaps my first lessons in the law and politics of U.S. regulatory regimes affecting international trade and business. Other events beyond my control that advanced my international awareness while at Commerce included passage of the Foreign Corrupt Practices Act, the imposition of sanctions in response to the Iranian hostage crisis, the U.S. embargo of the Olympics, and initial trade negotiations with China. When I left the government late at night January 19th, 1981, I left with the odd notion of wanting to start an international practice, maybe one that would bring together elements of international work that, up until that time, had tended to be in separate firms or, at best, in separate, unconnected parts of the same large firm.

In reflecting on having migrated from that point in time—early 1981—to finding myself in 2007 as a surprisingly senior partner in the extraordinary law firm of Miller & Chevalier, I can perhaps offer a few observations. One is that it would make good sense for anyone interested in international law to do many of the things I did not do. Spending time abroad, seeing the United States from the outside in, learning foreign languages, studying international law, finding out about civil law systems and Sharia courts, being a conspicuous minority in a culture different from your own—all these are valuable experiences for anyone whose future legal practice is likely to involve clients, laws, and legal problems that span more than one culture.

It is undoubtedly also helpful to be prepared to be professionally nimble. None of the areas of the law on which I now focus my practice and through which I earn a living was a subject that was taught when I was in law school. Most didn't exist at all, or at least not in a recognizably similar form. For anyone who is reading this piece without the aid of reading glasses, the pace of substantive change in legal specialties in the future is likely to be even faster than it was for me. (This reality also reinforces my abiding bias that law school is really about learning to think, analyze, write, and advocate, and not about substantive learning.)

Another comforting proposition, particularly in the face of not knowing what your legal specialty may be in a few years, is that there is some value in becoming expert in small things. Glacial professional forces are putting a premium on specialization. What they also enable, however, is the likes of any of us to learn quite a lot about—and become relatively expert in—particular small topics. For example, knowing everything there is to know about "reportable requests" under the Commerce Department's anti-boycott law may not be a universally prized asset, but it may well be of intense interest to certain paying clients and will add an identifiable badge to one's professional profile.

Small opportunities can also lead in unexpected directions. My unintended entry into the world of the ABA could be traced to a request in the early 1980s that I prepare a draft report and resolution for the International Section on the extraterritorial application of U.S. export controls laws. This was a subject about which I had not yet forgotten what I had learned in government and on which I could easily gather a few others who knew quite a lot. Over two or three brown bag lunches, we prepared a draft and then watched it bob along through the various channels of the ABA's bureaucracy until it actually was approved as formal ABA policy by a large sea of faces that I later came to know as the ABA House of Delegates. This small project, possibly together with low expectations that we would ever produce a draft, was my first step onto the slippery slope of participation in the ABA.

Through the ABA, I have come to appreciate that bar associations can be congenial venues for professional and educational experiments. One small but enduring example in my career dates from the mid-1980s when, as a new ABA trade committee desperately seeking to make our way, some one of us thought that we might call an early breakfast program "Breakfast at the Bar," a format that stuck and continues to this day. Likewise, the "Practitioners' Workshop"—so labeled, as I recall, primarily because we didn't intend to serve breakfast—has survived. And the ever-successful John Jackson mini-course on the WTO—then on the GATT—that we first offered at the Wye Plantation at about the same time continues to be one of the CLE jewels of the Section. I believe that it was the first of these that attracted Jonathan Fried, later to become the National Security Adviser to the Prime Minister of Canada, and Grant Aldonas, later to become Under Secretary of Commerce for International Trade, amongst others. But then again, with John Jackson as the impresario, how could those seminars have been anything other than highly successful?

Uncertain projects can also sometimes lead far beyond their original horizons. I was fortunate in the late 1980s to be able to collaborate with Sandy D'Alemberte, an indefatigable, effervescent source of innovative ideas, both as ABA president and otherwise. He encouraged and guided my improbable idea of a large, bilateral conference of American and Soviet lawyers in the then still-communist Soviet Union. The idea got traction, and the unlikely result was the 1990 Moscow Conference, attended by over two thousand American and Soviet lawyers and judges who met in the Kremlin to discuss 32 topics, some of the provocative ones of which had never before been publicly addressed in the Soviet Union. The negotiated conference schedule included a morning break to allow attendees to attend Rosh Hashanah services (a radical notion in the Soviet Union in 1990), an impromptu 30-minute soliloquy by a beleaguered Michal Gorbachev, and a final banquet above the massive Palace of Congresses, complete with a blues singer from New Orleans and dancing, both of which were firsts for that building.

The Moscow conference, which commands only a modest note in the Section's archives, gave impetus, in turn, to the idea of the Central and East European Law Initiative (CEELI), launched by the Section following the fall of the Berlin Wall. Born despite deep skepticism by both the U.S. State Department and the Board of Governors of the ABA, that uncertain project survived and ultimately flourished, continuing today in more than 25 countries. Like so many projects that ultimately do well, CEELI's success can be explained only by our good fortune in enlisting talented, dedicated volunteers. Among CEELI's pantheon of heroes: Mark Ellis, CEELI's first Executive Director, who masterfully guided its growth; Justice Sandra Day O'Connor, who has become a global leader for the rule of law; the beloved and sagacious Ambassador Max Kampelman; Judge Pat Wald, who must have traveled to the region 20 or more times; Abner Mikva, whose experience and insights span all three branches of government; and many others. They, in turn, helped inspire more than 5,000 lawyers and judges who have given freely of their time to help advance the law reform process in emerging democracies.

There are many examples of the extraordinary opportunities that pro bono work can offer in terms of professional development, satisfaction, and making a difference. Pro bono work afforded me my first civilian jury trial, a Mississippi voting rights case, a Supreme Court argument, and a front row seat for the historic transition of more than 25 former communist countries. Firms like Miller & Chevalier that support pro bono efforts deserve more credit than they get (my CEELI hours probably total between four and five work years), even when some of those hours come on top of billable work. Working with CEELI—some unpaid volunteers served three or four years in the field—profoundly affected the careers and priorities of scores of lawyers and judges, many of whom point to their experiences in the field as the most rewarding of their professional lives. That this pro bono work so enriched the lives of the volunteers was an unintended but magnificent side effect of the historic work that those volunteers did and continue to do.

Both the Moscow conference and CEELI hold multiple lessons: that the potential rewards of taking occasional risks (both institutional and individual) can be substantial; that small ideas and opportunities often lead down unpredictable paths; that collaborating with smart, dedicated, visionary colleagues can be the key to success; that serving the public good remains a powerful impulse among American lawyers; and that the rule of law (a phrase that, as Justice Kennedy points out, our generation never heard mentioned in law school) is vitally important in parts of the world where it remains an unrealized ideal, not a slogan or something we take for granted. It is also enlightening and humbling to gain an appreciation of the immense challenges faced by some of our professional colleagues elsewhere in the world.

Lest this piece become more avuncular than intended, it may be appropriate to take a moment also to applaud the importance of periodic silliness and irreverence, and the laughter they engender. All my favorite lawyers have had a ready laugh. If one happens to spend extended time in Washington, irreverence should begin to come naturally—and remind us of how far we have to go in being high-minded and public-spirited in tending to the public's business. Silliness is more personal. And not without its own risks.

At a black-tie dinner of Covington & Burling lawyers in about 1974, two highly naïve associates—the other was named David Brown—found themselves standing at the back of the crowded room nervously holding guitars. Realizing that singing at a formal Covington lawyers dinner (at which the featured speaker was the quintessentially dignified former Secretary of Defense, Clark Clifford) was not only unprecedented, but possibly foolhardy, David—after it was far too late—whispered, "Homer, this could be a terrible mistake." As the partner-emcee re-directed the gaze of the unsuspecting diners to the rear of the room, we launched into two songs, the first parodying the firm's feared and revered senior partner, Tommy Austern, and the other making fun of the firm's recruiting strategy of taking law student recruits to extravagant restaurants with menus most law students couldn't read. Not knowing how to react to such a preposterous stunt, the audience responded not by the death-sentence stony silence we feared, but by standing and applauding.

It probably does not reflect well on one's legal career to name as one of its highlights being applauded by more than 100 distinguished lawyers for singing two silly songs written to tunes by John Prine. But it is what it is, and David Brown and I are still friends. So, too, are the members of that 1975 dinner committee who approved our nonsense in advance: Paul Tagliabue, who later became commissioner of the NFL, and Tom Williamson, who has always wanted just to play in the NFL.

The truth is that there were other moments of silly singing (for which the element of surprise is essential, unless you enlist really good singers, like Ricki Tigert, who later became general counsel of the Fed instead). At the Section's first retreat at Amelia Island in 1991, we pilloried in song Ken Reisenfeld's fantasy that the Section hold meetings in Europe (something the Section now does regularly). At Jim Silkenat's instigation at a later retreat, for which I had no responsibility, a very small group of us wound through the audience singing and pantomiming some version of "YMCA." And upon the retirement of Edison Dick, the venerable director of the Section's International Legal Exchange trips for a generation, whose red sport coat we borrowed for the occasion, we sang "I've Got the Trip for You," to a tune stolen from "Guys and Dolls." The lyrics may have been some of my best legal writing.

When doing silly things—not all of which are universally welcomed—it is helpful to keep in mind that not all mistakes and gaffes are career-ending (although, alas, some may be). A public slip of the tongue, an unflattering press item, an argument that a judge excoriates, an ill-timed joke, a demoralizing critique by a senior partner, a futile cold call that still makes you cringe, an email *about* a client inadvertently sent *to* a client—most of these embarrassing occasions are not fatal, but are simply collected in that mental bin of things that you recall only when you wake up during the night. We all know of incidents that we treasure, such as a former colleague who got on the shuttle from New York to Washington and discovered en route that the ocean was on the right side of the plane and, therefore, that Boston, not Washington, lay ahead; or another who appeared for an important oral argument, removed his topcoat, and learned that his suit coat was back in Washington; or a third who distracted himself outside the courthouse before argument by whistling at a nearby passerby who turned out to be the judge in his case. Episodes such as these (only a couple of which are autobiographical), are character-building, although that insight comes only with the passage of time.

Finally, I believe it is healthy to keep in mind that practicing law is not the be-all-and-end-all in life, even when it claims to be. Resisting the voracious appetite that the law business has for one's personal time is not easy. However, life's greatest satisfactions are found in neither the marginal billable hour nor the marginal dollar of compensation. Most are found in diversions and other interests, be they family, music, high mountain ranges, or low-brow novels (Carl Hiaasen, for example). Smelling flowers and planting trees are worthy endeavors. Learning to use the technology that now stalks us around the clock to gain more time and flexibility has also become a valuable professional skill. And, of course, we all have happy colleagues who, to paraphrase John Kennedy's slanderous comment about the advantages of a Harvard education and a Yale degree, have combined the rewards of a legal education and a non-legal career. (In recently calling law school classmates for reunion gifts, in quick succession I came upon a priest, a college president, a Wyoming politician, a New York artist, and one adventuresome friend whose career path remains undocumented.)

My advice to any readers who may still be with us is to read the foregoing not for advice or guidance, but as one example of a non-linear legal career that has proved rewarding and enjoyable, much as you might read an obituary of someone you don't know but whose life experiences may cause you to reflect on how you might wish to map your own. Then, if you have a few remaining moments of free time, you could read a poem. Poems by Billy Collins are terrific, and often make you laugh.

Appendix
Studying Abroad

A

The American Bar Association's *Standards for the Approval of Law Schools* provides in Standard 307 that an ABA-approved law school may grant credit for studies or activities in a foreign country only for studies or activities that have been approved in accordance with the Rules of Procedure and Criteria adopted by the ABA Council on Legal Education. Outside of programs that meet these criteria, an ABA-approved law school may not award credit toward the J.D. degree to an enrolled student for studies or activities outside of the United States.

J.D. students at ABA-approved law schools who want to receive credit toward their J.D. degrees for foreign study should read the requirements for their course of study and should consult with law school faculty and staff who advise students about foreign study opportunities.

Under the rules for ABA-approved law schools, foreign study programs are open only to those students who have successfully completed their first year of law school (i.e., two semesters) and are in good academic standing. These students have three options for foreign study programs that they can count toward their J.D. degrees. These three options are:

- An ABA-approved foreign summer program
- An ABA-approved semester abroad program
- A school approved individual study program, sometimes done in cooperation with an ABA-approved cooperative program between and ABA-approved law school and a foreign institution

These options reflect the belief of the Council on Legal Education that foreign study programs and opportunities have value to law students, the law schools, and the legal profession. New criteria to approve foreign programs became effective in 2003 to take into account the many emerging ways that law schools are using to expand the availability of foreign study opportunities.

Contact your school's financial aid office for information on financial assistance not only for tuition, but also for assistance with the cost of travel and foreign housing.

A. Foreign Summer Programs

The current list of ABA-approved foreign summer programs can be found at http://www.abanet.org/legaled/studyabroad/foreign.html. Contact each law school directly for information on the dates of each program, the costs of tuition, housing, and other fees, application deadlines, and specific courses offered. Before signing up for any program, check with your own school to be sure that credits earned in the foreign program can be applied to the requirements of your degree.

SCHOOL	PROGRAM LOCATION
Akron, University of	Geneva, Switzerland
Alabama, University of	Canberra, Australia
Alabama, University of	Fribourg, Switzerland
American University	Santiago, Chile / Buenos Aires, Argentina

SCHOOL	PROGRAM LOCATION
American University	Paris/Geneva/Barcelona/London
American University	The Hague, The Netherlands
American University	Hong Kong
American University	Paris and Nanterre, France
American University	Istanbul, Turkey
Arkansas, University of	St. Petersburg, Russia
Baltimore, University of	Aberdeen, Scotland
Baltimore, University of	Chile, Argentina
Baltimore, University of	Curacao, Netherland Antilles
Baltimore, University of	Haifa, Israel
Baylor University	Guadalajara, Mexico
Boston College	London, England
Boston University	Oxford, England
Brooklyn Law School	Beijing, China
California Western	Wellington, New Zealand
California Western	Tijuana, Mexico/Toronto, Canada
California-Hastings, University of	The Netherlands
Campbell University	Handong, South Korea
Catholic University of America	Cracow, Poland
Columbia University	University of Amsterdam
Columbia University	University of Paris, France
Columbia University	Buenos Aires, Argentina
Connecticut, University of	University of Exeter, Devon/ University of London, U.K. Leiden University, The Netherlands
Cornell University	Paris, France
Cornell University	Berlin, Germany
Cornell University	Suzhou, China
DePaul University	Bejiing, China
DePaul University	San Jose, Costa Rica
DePaul University	Dublin, Ireland
Drake University	Nantes, France
Duke University	Geneva, Switzerland

SCHOOL	PROGRAM LOCATION
Duke University	Hong Kong
Duquesne University	Beijing, China
Duquesne University	Rome, Italy
Duquesne University	Dublin, Ireland
Florida, University of	The Netherlands
Florida Coastal	Clermont-Ferrand, France
Florida International	Seville, Spain
Florida State University	Oxford, England
Fordham University	Belfast/Dublin, Ireland
Fordham University	Seoul, Korea
Franklin Pierce Law Center	Beijing, China
Franklin Pierce Law Center	Cork, Ireland
Georgetown University	London, England
Georgetown University	Fribourg, Switzerland
Georgia, University of	Oxford, England
Georgia, University of	Beijing/Shanghai, China
Georgia, University of	Brussels, Belgium
Georgia State University	Linz, Austria
Georgia State University	Rio de Janiero, Brazil
George Washington University	Munich, Germany
George Washington University	Oxford, England
Golden Gate University	Bangkok, Thailand
Golden Gate University	Paris, France
Gonzaga University	Florence, Italy
Hamline University	Oslo/Bergen, Norway
Hamline University	Jerusalem, Israel/San Juan, Puerto Rico/ London, England
Hamline University	Paris, France / Budapest, Hungary
Hamline University	Rome, Italy
Hofstra University	Nice, France
Hofstra University	Curacao, Netherland Antilles
Hofstra University	Sydney, Australia

SCHOOL	PROGRAM LOCATION
Hofstra University	Sorrento, Italy
Howard University	Cape Town, South Africa
Illinois, University of	Oxford, England
Indiana University - Indianapolis	Strasbourg, France
Indiana University - Indianapolis	Beijing, China
Indiana University - Indianapolis	La Plata, Argentina
Indiana University - Indianapolis	Dubrovnik, Croatia
Inter American University of Puerto Rico	Beijing, China
Inter American University of Puerto Rico	London, England
Inter American University of Puerto Rico	Venice, Italy
Inter American University of Puerto Rico	Madrid, Spain
Iowa, University of	Arcachon, France
Kansas, University of	Istanbul, Turkey
Kansas, University of	Limerick, Ireland
Louisiana State University	Lyon, France
Louisiana State University	Buenos Aires, Argentina
Loyola Law School - Los Angeles	Bologna, Italy
Loyola Law School - Los Angeles	Ciudad Colon, Costa Rica
Loyola Law School - Los Angeles	Beijing China
Loyola University - Chicago	Oxford, Strasbourg, Luxembourg, Brussels
Loyola University - Chicago	Rome, Italy
Loyola University - New Orleans	Vienna, Austria
Loyola University - New Orleans	Rio de Janiero, Brazil
Loyola University - New Orleans	Cuernavaca, Mexico
Loyola University - New Orleans	Moscow, Russia
Loyola University - New Orleans	Budapest, Hungary
Loyola University - New Orleans	San Jose, Costa Rica
Marquette University	Queensland, Australia
Marquette University	Brisbane, Australia
Maryland, University of	Aberdeen, Scotland
McGeorge School of Law	London, England

SCHOOL	PROGRAM LOCATION
McGeorge School of Law	Salzburg, Austria
McGeorge School of Law	Suzhou, China
Miami, University of	London, England
Miami, University of	Madrid/Fuengirola/Seville, Spain
Miami, University of	Athens/Mykonos/Corfu, Greece
Michigan, University of	The Netherlands
Michigan, University of	London, England
Michigan, University of	Geneva, Switzerland
Michigan State University	Ottawa, Canada
Michigan State University	Guadalajara/Zapopan/Jalisco, Mexico
Minnesota, University of	Beijing, China
Minnesota, University of	University of Uppsala, Sweden
Missouri-Kansas City, University of	Dingle/Galway/Dublin, Ireland
Missouri-Kansas City, University of	Beijing, China
Missouri - Columbia, University of	Cape Town, South Africa
Mississippi University	Cambridge, England
New England School of Law	Galway, Ireland
New Mexico, University of	Guanajuato, Mexico
North Carolina, University of	Sydney, Australia
North Dakota, University of	Oslo, Norway
Northern Illinois University	Agen, France
Notre Dame	London, England
Northwestern University	London, England
Ohio State University	Oxford, England
Oklahoma City University	Tianjin, China
Oklahoma University of	Oxford, England
Pace University	London, England
Pennsylvania State	Florence/Rome/Sienna, Italy
Pennsylvania State	Capitals of Europe: Strasbourg, France/ Brussels, Belgium/Vienna, Austria/ The Hague, The Netherlands/ Oxford, England
Pennsylvania State	Montreal, Canada

SCHOOL	PROGRAM LOCATION
Pepperdine University	London, England
Pepperdine University	Hong Kong
Pittsburgh, University of	Pacific Rim
Puerto Rico, University of	Barcelona, Spain
Puerto Rico, University of	Santiago, Chile
Quinnipiac University	Dublin, Ireland
Regent University	Strasbourg, France
Richmond, University of	Cambridge, England
Roger Williams University	Lisbon, Portugal
Roger Williams University	London, England
Rutgers University - Newark	The Netherlands
Saint Louis University	Madrid, Spain
Saint Louis University	Berlin, Germany
Samford University	Durham, England
Samford University	Victoria, British Columbia
Samford University	Fortaleza, Brazil
San Diego, University of	Barcelona, Spain
San Diego, University of	Dublin, Ireland
San Diego, University of	Florence, Italy
San Diego, University of	London, England
San Diego, University of	Oxford, England
San Diego, University of	Paris, France
San Diego, University of	Moscow/St. Petersburg, Russia
San Francisco, University of	Bali, Indonesia
San Francisco, University of	Budapest, Hungary
San Francisco, University of	Dublin, Ireland
San Francisco, University of	Prague, Czech Republic
Santa Clara University	Istanbul, Turkey
Santa Clara University	Hong Kong/Shanghai
Santa Clara University	Munich, Germany
Santa Clara University	Austria/Slovakia/Hungary
Santa Clara University	Oxford, England

SCHOOL	PROGRAM LOCATION
Santa Clara University	Singapore/Thailand/Vietnam/Cambodia
Santa Clara University	Tokyo, Japan
Santa Clara University	Seoul, South Korea
Santa Clara University	Sydney, Australia
Santa Clara University	Geneva, Switzerland/Strasbourg, France
Santa Clara University	The Hague, The Netherlands
Santa Clara University	San Jose, Costa Rica
Seattle University	Johannesburg, South Africa
Seton Hall University	Milan/Parma/Rapallo, Italy
Seton Hall University	Cairo, Egypt
Seton Hall University	Galway, Ireland/Leuven, Belgium
Seton Hall University	Zanzibar, Tanzania
South Carolina	London, England
South Texas	Valletta, Malta
South Texas	The Netherlands
South Texas	University of Aarhus, Denmark
South Texas	Prague, Czech Republic
Southern Methodist University	Oxford, England
Southern University	London, England
Southwestern University	Cambridge, England
Southwestern University	Vancouver, British Columbia
Southwestern University	Buenos Aires, Argentina
Southwestern University	London, England
Southwestern University	Guanajuato, Mexico
St. John's University	Rome, Italy
St. Mary's University	Innsbruck, Austria
St. Thomas University	San Lorenzo de El Escorial, Spain
St. Thomas, University of	Rome, Italy (conjunction with Villanova)
Stetson University	Granada, Spain
Stetson University	Buenos Aires, Argentina
Stetson University	Freiburg, Germany/The Hague, The Netherlands

SCHOOL	PROGRAM LOCATION
Suffolk University	Lund, Sweden
Syracuse University	London, England
Temple University	Rome, Italy
Temple University	Tokyo, Japan
Texas, University of	London, England
Thomas Jefferson School of Law	Hangzhou, China
Thomas M. Cooley Law School	Toronto, Canada
Thomas M. Cooley Law School	Melbourne, Australia/Christchurch, New Zealand
Touro College	Moscow, Russia
Touro College	Potsdam/Berlin, Germany
Touro College	Shimla, India
Touro College	Xiamen, China
Touro College	Jerusalem, Israel
Tulane University	Rhodos/Spetes, Greece
Tulane University	Amsterdam, The Netherlands
Tulane University	Berlin, Germany
Tulane University	Buenos Aires, Argentina
Tulane University	London, England
Tulsa, University of	London, England
Tulsa, University of	Dublin, Ireland
Tulsa, University of	Geneva, Switzerland
Valparaiso University	Cambridge/London, England
Valparaiso University	Santiago, Chile/ Buenos Aires, Argentina
Vanderbilt University	Venice Italy
Villanova University	Rome, Italy (conjunction with U. of St. Thomas)
Wake Forest University	London, England
Wake Forest University	Venice, Italy
Wake Forest University	Vienna, Austria
Washburn University	Utrecht, The Netherlands
Washington University (St. Louis)	Utrecht, The Netherlands

SCHOOL	PROGRAM LOCATION
Whittier	Amsterdam, The Netherlands
Whittier	Ramat Gan, Israel
Whittier	Santander, Spain
Whittier	Toulouse, France
Whittier	Zhuhai, China
Widener University	Geneva, Switzerland
Widener University	Nairobi, Kenya
Widener University	Sydney, Australia
Widener University	Venice, Italy
Willamette University	Hamburg, Germany
Willamette University	Shanghai, China
William Mitchell	Edinburgh, Scotland/London, England
William and Mary	Madrid, Spain
Wisconsin, University of	The Netherlands
Yeshiva University	Paris, France/Budapest, Hungary

B.   Semester Study Abroad Programs

Some schools offer the possibility of spending an entire semester abroad. A current list of law schools that offer such programs (either individually or in cooperation with other law schools) can be found at http://www.abanet.org/legaled/studyabroad/semester .html. Contact those schools directly for information on course offerings, registration deadlines, and application procedures. Be sure to check well in advance that your home law school will accept all of the credits earned in a foreign semester study programs.

SCHOOL	PROGRAM LOCATION
Chicago-Kent College of Law, Indiana University-Bloomington, University of Iowa, University of Kansas, University of Missouri-Columbia, and the University of Utah (the "London Law Consortium")	London, England [Spring Semester]

SCHOOL	PROGRAM LOCATION
Boston College Law School (available only to Boston College students)	London, England [Spring Semester]
University of Detroit Mercy School of Law	London, England [Fall and Spring Semesters]
Notre Dame Law School (available only to Notre Dame students)	London, England [Fall and Spring Semesters]
Pace University School of Law	London, England [Spring Semester]
Pepperdine University School of Law	London, England [Fall Semester]
Temple University School of Law	Tokyo, Japan [Spring Semester]
Thomas M. Cooley Law School	Melbourne, Australia and Christchurch, New Zealand [Spring Semester]
University of Tulsa College of Law	London, England [Fall Semester]

C. Foreign Cooperative Study Programs

Many law schools have programs in which they cooperate with foreign law schools and other institutions to provide a wide variety of educational and training opportunities. The exact nature of each cooperative program varies from school to school and from country to country. Contact each school directly for more information on the various programs. A current list of ABA-approved programs can be found at http://www.abanet.org/legaled/studyabroad/coop.html.

SCHOOL	PROGRAM LOCATION
American University	Hong Kong
American University	Paris, France
Boston University	Oxford, England
Boston College	Oxford, England
California Western	Wellington, New Zealand
California-Hasting, University of	British Columbia,Canada
California-Hasting, University of	Netherlands
Campbell University	Handong, South Korea
Columbia University	Hamburg, Germany

SCHOOL	PROGRAM LOCATION
Columbia University	Amsterdam, Netherlands
Columbia University	Paris, France
Connecticut University	London, England
Connecticut University	Exeter, England
Connecticut University	Leiden, England
Cornell University	London, England
Cornell University	Paris, France
Cornell University	Berlin, Germany
DePaul University	Dublin, Ireland
Emory University	Hamburg, Germany
Florida University of Levin	Frankfurt, Germany
Fordham University	Amsterdam, Netherlands
Georgetown University	Fribourg, Switzerland
George Mason University	Hamburg, Germany
Inter American University of Puerto Rico	Madrid, Spain
Michigan State University	Ottawa, Canada
Michigan, University of	Leiden, Netherlands
Michigan, University of	London, England
Minnesota, University of	Uppsala, Sweden
New Mexico, University of	Ottawa, Canada
New Mexico, University of	Tasmania
New Mexico, University of	Ontario, Canada
New York University	Amsterdam, Netherlands
North Carolina, University of	Niijemgen, Netherlands
North Carolina, University of	Iberoamericana
North Carolina, University of	Lyon, France
North Carolina, University of	Glasgow, Scotland
North Carolina, University of	Manchester, England
North Dakota, University of	Oslo, Norway
Puerto Rico University	Santiago, Chile
Puerto Rico University	Barcelona, Spain
South Texas	Aarhus, Denmark

SCHOOL	PROGRAM LOCATION
Texas at Austin, University of	London, England
Tulane University	Buenos Aires, Argentina
Tulsa, University of	Hamburg, Germany
Vermont Law School	McGill, Montreal
Virginia, University of	Hamburg, Germany
Willamette University	Hamburg, Germany
Wisconsin, University of	Florence, Italy
Wisconsin, University of	Netherlands
Yeshivia University	Hamburg, Germany

Appendix B
Internet Resources
compiled by Alina Huiu

These Web sites are only a starting point in your pursuit of an international legal career.

Federal Government–Related Web Sites
www.usda.gov Department of Agriculture
www.ogc.doc.gov Department of Commerce
www.doe.gov Department of Energy
www.usdoj.gov Department of Justice
www.dol.gov Department of Labor
www.state.gov/careers Department of State
www.treas.gov/jobs Department of the Treasury
www.epa.gov Environmental Protection Agency
www.exim.gov Export-Import Bank of the United States
www.fcc.gov/jobs Federal Communications Commission
www.ftc.gov Federal Trade Commission
www.fda.gov Food & Drug Administration
www.ins.org Immigration and Naturalization Service
www.nasa.gov National Aeronautics and Space Administration
www.uspto.gov Patent & Trademark Office
www.ustr.gov/ Office of the U.S. Trade Representative
www.opic.gov Overseas Private Investment Corporation (OPIC)

www.sec.gov Securities & Exchange Commission

www.usaid.gov U.S. Agency for International Development

http://www.cit.uscourts.gov/ U.S. Court of International Trade

www.usitc.gov U.S. International Trade Commission

International Web Sites

www.interaction.org/jobs Web site of the American Council for Voluntary International Action; lists job resources, internship and volunteer opportunities, and position openings (by subscription) in international development organizations.

www.aals.org Association of American Law Schools; provides information on law faculty positions.

www.ecojobs.com Environmental career opportunities

www.iadb.org Inter-American Development Bank

www.icnl.org International Center for Not-for-Profit Law

www.icrc.org International Committee of the Red Cross

www.ifc.org International Finance Corporation

http://hrlawgroup.org/ International Human Rights Law Group

www.ilo.org International Labour Organization; has Young Professionals and internship programs.

www.lawgazette.co.uk A publication of the Law Society of England and Wales that features online job searches.

www.lawsoc.org.uk Law Society of England and Wales; lists positions available at the Law Society.

www.oas.org Organization of American States

www.owit.org Organization of Women in International Trade; can browse a list of current job openings but need subscription for full descriptions.

www.pslawnet.org The Public Service Law Network Worldwide (PSLawNet) is a global network of some 190 member law schools and nearly 11,000 law-related public service organizations and offices around the world. To that end, PSLawNet offers information on a broad range of pro bono and public service opportunities.

www.rightsinternational.org Web site for the Center for Human Rights Law includes information on internship and other programs.

https://jobs.un.org/elearn/production/home.html Employment Web site of the United Nations www.worldbank.org The World Bank

www.iucn.org The World Conservation Union

www.wipo.org World Intellectual Property Organization

www.wto.org World Trade Organization

Legal Career Web Sites

http://jobline.acc.com/ Interactive employment service of the Association of Corporate Counsel.

www.attorneyjobs.com   Lists attorney jobs in the United States and abroad.

www.emplawyernet.com

www.hg.org

www.job-hunt.org/law.shtml

jobs.lawinfo.com

www.lawbulletin.com Publishers of the *Chicago Daily Law Bulletin;* can search job ads online.

www.lawjobs.com

legalemploy.com Provides links to legal-related employment.

Index

A

ABA Central European and
Eurasian Law Initiative
(CEELI), 151–153, 156,
201–202
ABA House of Delegates, 200
*ABA International Lawyer's
Deskbook*, 171
ABA Rule of Law Initiative
(ROLI), 156–157, 159
Accounting, experience in, 31
Ad hoc international
institution, 134
Ad hoc tribunals, 112, 113,
114, 115, 117, 120,
121, 122
Adaptability, 15, 135
Admirality & Shipping
Section, 80
Admirality practice, 79–83
advantages of, 81–83
disadvantages of, 81
introduction to, 79–81

starting out in, 83
training for, 83
ADRs. *See* American Depositary
Receipts (ADRs)
Advocacy skills, 132
Africa, 15, 55, 156
African Development Bank, 158
Age, 56
Alaska, 29, 30
Aldonas Grant, 201
Allen & Overy LLP, 4, 5–6, 184
Alumni Office, 179
American Arbitration
Association, 166
American Bar Association, 7,
177, 188, 198, 200, 201
American Depositary Receipts
(ADRs), 31
*American Review of
International Arbitration*,
98, 107
American Society of
International Law, 98, 123

American Society of
International Law and
Amnesty International, 118
AMEX International, Inc., 157
Amnesty International, 123
Anti-boycott law, 199, 200
Appeals unit, ICTY and, 116
Arbitral tribunal, 99, 101
Arbitration International, 98, 107
ARD. *See* Associates in Rural
Development, Inc. (ARD)
Aresty, Jeffrey M., 163
Argentina, 42–43, 139
Argentine Foreign Affairs
department, 42
Asia, 8, 55, 58, 156, 193
Asia Development Bank, 158
Asia Foundation, 157
Asian Institute of International
Financial Law (AIIFL), 92
Associates in Rural
Development, Inc.
(ARD), 157
Association of Corporate
Counsel chapter, 67
Associations
China and, 93–94
joining, 20–21
AT&T, 85
Attorney, international rule of
law. *See* International rule
of law attorney
Attorney-client
communication, 185
Australia, 9, 23, 65, 66, 80
Avocat, 12, 13, 14
AXENT Technologies, Inc., 59
Axtell, Roger, 185

B

Balance, 65, 143–145
Bar associations, 177–178, 179
Being and Nothingness, 28
Bender, Matthew, 14
Benefits, 145
*Best Lawyers in America,
The*, 83
Big/large firms, 35, 37
Bilateral contracts, 7
Black's Law Dictionary, 181
Blaškic trial, 121
Blogs, 170, 193
Blue Nile, 165
Body language, 24
Bombau, Marcelo, 41
Bosnia, 111, 134
Boston, 50, 170–171
Brand, personal, 192–194
Branding, 93–94
Brazil, 26, 36
"Breakfast at the Bar," 200
Breines, Andrew, 163
Breyer, Stephen, 55
British Columbia International
Arbitration Center, 108
British Commonwealth, 107
Brussels, 55
Buergenthal, Thomas, 55
Bulgaria, 152, 153
Burgundy, 15
Burke, Michael E., 85
Burma, 141
Burman, Harold, 55
Business communities, 44
Business unit management,
for international in-house
legal career, 68–70

C

Calling, career or, 131–132
Cambodian National
Assembly, 133
Canada, 23, 80
Canada Free Trade Agreement,
139
Capital costs, netting and, 10
Carana Corporation, 157
Career
in admirality practice (*See*
Admirality practice)
climbing ladder in, 190–194
diverse experience and, 23
in international commercial
arbitration (*See*
International commercial
arbitration)
in international criminal
law (*See* International
criminal law)
of international derivatives
lawyer, 3–10
international in-house legal
(*See* International in-
house legal career)
as international judge,
125–135
in international law, 12,
17–19, 33, 37–39,
131–135, 133, 186–190
in international trade law
(*See* International trade
law)
as Latin-American
transactional lawyer,
33–40
non-linear, 197–205

in small-firm international
law practice (*See* Small-
firm international law
practice)
Career Services Office, 175,
176, 179
Careers in International Law, 33
Caribbean, 156
Carter Administration, 199
Casals and Associates, Inc., 157
CEELI. *See* ABA Central
European and Eurasian
Law Initiative (CEELI)
Central Intelligence Agency,
185
Chambers, ICTY and, 113, 114
Chambers Legal Support
Unit, 114
Chambers of Commerce, 44, 68
Chambers USA Guide, 83
Chaplin, Charlie, 32
Chartered Institute of
Arbitrators, 98, 107
Checchi and Company,
Consulting, 157
Chemonics International,
Inc., 157
Cherry-picking, 10
Chicago, 173
Child care
in France, 19
international trade law and,
144–145
Children's Law Society, 177
China, 85–94, 142
China Committee, 92, 93
China Law Blog, 193
China law expert, 193

China Practice Group, 94
Choices
    job, 20
    lifestyle, 18–19
Civil law, 100
Claim Room, The, 165
CLE program. *See* Continuing legal education (CLE) program
Clerkship, 35, 105
Client development, 191
Clients
    foreign, 167–169, 192
    international in-house legal career and, 72
    research, 192
    success with, 15
Coast Guard, 83
Cohen, Michael Marks, 79
College, cultures and, 87
Commerce Department, 17, 138, 141, 142, 144, 200. *See also* U.S. Department of Commerce
Commercial law, 14
Committee, 178
Common Law, The, 28
Communication
    attorney-client, 185
    international criminal law and, 121, 123
    small-firm international law practice and, 170, 171
    telephone, 168
    verbal, 24
Communication skills, 121
Communications tools, 170
Community service, 68

Comparative law, 139
Competence, cross-cultural, 185
Compromises, in job choices, 20
Congress, 143
Connecting, 194
Connections, international criminal law and, 120
Conseil juridique, 12, 13
Contact book, 23
Contacts, international, 45
Continuing legal education (CLE) program, 178, 186
Contract(s)
    bilateral, 7
    derivative as, 7
    experience in, 31
    international, 45
    international commercial arbitration and, 97
    private, 7
Corell, Hans, 55
Corporate Counsel Committee of the American Arbitration Association, 98
Corporate law, 14, 31, 171
Costs, capital, 10
Counsel
    global, 57–58
    outside, 72–74
Court of Appeals for the Federal Circuit, 180
Court of International Trade, 173–174, 180
Covington & Burling, 198, 203
Cravath, Swaine & Moore, 4, 5

Creative Associates
International, 157
Credit risk, netting and, 10
Crime of aggression, 113
Crimes
for international criminal
law, 113, 135
organized, 128
war, 113, 128, 133
Crimes against humanity, 113,
120, 133
Criminal Code for the Socialist
Federal Republic of
Yugoslavia, 129
Criminal law reform,
international rule of law
attorney and, 155
Criminal Procedural Code for
SFRY, 129
Croatia, 153
*Crosby v. National Foreign
Trade Council*, 141
Cross-cultural competence, 185
Cultures, 23–24, 31–32, 34, 44,
66, 185, 189–190, 192
college and, 87
international criminal law
and, 120
small-firm international
law practice and,
170–171
Cunningham, Dan, 4
Current events, 179–180
Customs and Border
Protection, 147
Cyber law, 165
Cyber lawyers, 166–167
Cybersettle, 166

D

Deal rooms, 170
Defense counsel, ICTY and, 116
Delaware, 36–37
Dell, 58, 67
Democracy International,
Inc., 157
Department head, 72
Department of Agriculture, 147
Department of Commerce,
146, 199
Department of Homeland
Security, 147
Department of Justice, 148
Department of Labor, 148
Department of State, 147
Department of the
Treasury, 147
Derivatives
defined, 7
netting and, 9–10
one-liners and, 9–10
OTC, 9, 10
reasons for, 8
relevancy of, 6–7
skills for, 8–9
d'Estaing, Valery Giscard, 55
Development Alternatives,
Inc., 157
Development Associates,
Inc., 157
Diplomatic work, of
international rule of law
attorney, 155–156
Disabled lawyers, international
trade law and, 143
District of Columbia, 144
Diversity, 15, 56, 83

Doing Business in France, 14
DPK Consulting, 157
Drug trafficking, 113, 128

E
East West Management
   Institute, 157
eBay, 165
E-books, 167
Echols, Marsha, 55
Ecuador, 25, 27, 28–29, 30
Education, 22, 132–133
Educational programs, 167
E-guides, 167
E-kits, 167
E-learning suites, 170
Electronic commerce, 171
E-mail, 168, 170, 185
E-mail relationships, 66
Embassy, 30
Employees
   international in-house legal
      career and, 71
   international trade law
      and, 145
Employer
   prospective, 178–179
   research, 189–190, 192
   résumé and, 174–177
Employment, federal, 145–146
England, 80
Enix-Ross, Deborah, 56
Environment
   global legal, 164–165
   international law and, 18
   working, 62
Environmental Law Society, 177

Environmental Protection
   Agency (EPA), 148
Europe, 11, 12, 34, 50, 55, 165
Executive Branch, 143
EXIM. *See* Export-Import Bank
   of the United States
   (EXIM)
Experience
   bolstering, 187–188
   hands-on, 35, 36
   international criminal law
      and, 121
Exporters, international trade
   law and, 141–142
Export-Import Bank of the
   United States (EXIM), 147
Extranets, 170
Extraordinary Chambers in
   the Courts of Cambodia,
   112, 133–134
Exxon Research and
   Engineering, 87

F
Family
   admirality practice and, 83
   expectations and, 20
   international trade law and,
      143–145
Family and Medical Leave
   Act (FMLA), 145
FCPA. *See* Foreign Corrupt
   Practices Act (FCPA)
Federal employment,
   disadvantages of, 145–146
Federal government, web sites
   for, 146–148, 221–222

Feedback, 193
Feinerman, Jim, 89
Feinstein, Dianne, 87
Fellowship examination, 98
Ferrazzi, Keith, 194
Field Mission Vacancy
    Notice, 130
Field Vacancy Notice, 128
Financial Markets International,
    Inc., 157
Financial Times, 180
Flexibility, 15, 61
Flexible work schedules, 144
FMLA. *See* Family and Medical
    Leave Act (FMLA)
Focus, 62
Food and Drug Administration
    (FDA), 148
Footsie 100, 8
Foreign Affairs, 180
Foreign clients
    cultivating, 192
    small-firm international
        law practice and,
        167–169
Foreign Corrupt Practices Act
    (FCPA), 140, 199
Foreign Policy, 180
France, labor laws in, 19
Friedman, Thomas, 184
Friends
    expectations and, 20
    as future, 38
    hiring, 72–73
Friendships, international
    criminal law and, 120
Fuld, Stanley H., 80

G

Gallucci, Dean Robert, 188
Gender, 56
Gender issues, international
    rule of law attorney
    and, 155
General Counsel, international
    in-house legal career and,
    74, 75, 76–77
Geneva, 106
Geneva Conventions, 133
Genocide, 113, 120, 133
*Gestures: The Do's and Taboos
    for Body Language around
    the World*, 185
Ghana, 134
Global awareness, 66
Global counsel, 57–58
Global cyber law, 164, 171
Global Internet telephony, 170
Global legal environment,
    164–165
Globalization, 30, 184–185, 190
Goals, 63, 68, 69, 70, 75, 190
Golden, Jeffrey B., 3
Goldstein, Marc J., 95
Gorbachev, Michel, 201
*Governing China: From
    Revolution Through
    Reform*, 87
Government National
    Mortgage Association, 138
Graduate school, international
    criminal law and,
    119–120
Granovetter, Mark, 188
Grossman, Dean Claudio, 55

H

Hague, The, 96–97, 115, 134
Hands-on experience, 35, 36
Hariri, Rafiq, 112, 134
Harris & Moure, PLLC, 193
Harris, Dan, 193
Herzegovina, 111, 134
Herzog, Carolyn, 57–77
Heston, Charleston, 76
Hieros Gamos web site, 188
Hiring, 72–73
Hispanic National Bar
    Association, 188
Holmes, Justice, 28
Homage to Catalonia, 26
Hong Kong, 80, 82, 92, 165
Hong Kong International
    Arbitration Center, 108
Horowitz, Bruce, 25
HUD. *See* U.S. Department of
    Housing and Urban
    Development (HUD)
Human Rights mitigation,
    international rule of law
    attorney and, 155
Human Rights Watch, 123
Humor, 32

I

IBO Institute, 163
IBRD. *See* International Bank
    for Reconstruction and
    Development (IBRD)
ICC. *See* International Chamber
    of Commerce (ICC);
    International Criminal
    Court (ICC)

ICC arbitration attorney, 13
ICC Bulletin, 99, 107
ICC Court of International
    Arbitration, 98–99
ICC Secretariat, 106
ICCA. *See* International
    Council on Commercial
    Arbitration (ICCA)
ICCA Congress Series, 99
*ICCA Yearbook on Commercial
    Arbitration*, 98, 107
ICTR. *See* International
    Criminal Tribunal for
    Rwanda (ICTR)
ICTs. *See* Information
    communications
    technologies (ICTs)
ICTY. *See* International
    Criminal Tribunal for the
    former Yugoslavia (ICTY)
IDA. *See* International
    Development Association
    (IDA)
IFES. *See* International
    Foundation for Election
    Systems (IFES)
ILEX. *See* International Legal
    Exchange (ILEX)
ILRC. *See* International Legal
    Assistance Resource Center
    (ILRC)
Immersion, international law
    and, 132
Immigrants, 29–30, 85
Independence, 14–16
Information communications
    technologies (ICTs), 165, 166

In-house legal career. *See*
International in-house
legal career
Instant messaging, 170
Institute for Transnational
Arbitration, 98, 107
Intellectual property laws, 171
Inter-American Development
Bank, 158
International Association of
Prosecutors, 123
International Bank for
Reconstruction and
Development (IBRD), 158
International Bar Association,
107, 188
International Business Law
Firm, The, 54
*International Chamber of
Commerce Bulletin*, 98
International Chamber of
Commerce (ICC), 13, 98,
106, 107
International commercial
arbitration, 95–108
career preparation advice
for, 105–108
choosing law firm and,
97–99
introduction to, 95–96
New York/Hague and,
96–97
rewards for, 99–105
International contacts, 45
International Council on
Commercial Arbitration
(ICCA), 98

International Courts
Committee, 123
International Criminal Court
(ICC), 17, 112, 122,
133, 134
International criminal law,
111–124
emerging system for,
112–113
ICTY and, 111–118, 122, 133
introduction to, 111–112
practical advice for,
118–123
International Criminal Law
Committee, 123
International Criminal Law
Society, 177
International Criminal Tribunal
for Rwanda (ICTR), 112,
113, 115, 122, 133
International Criminal
Tribunal for the former
Yugoslavia (ICTY),
111–118, 122, 133
International derivatives
lawyer, 3–10
International Development
Association (IDA), 158
International Dispute
Resolution Committee, 98
International Foundation
for Election Systems
(IFES), 157
International human rights,
principles of, 129
International humanitarian
law, 119

International in-house legal
  career, 57–78
  building relationships and,
    65–67
  business unit management
    and, 68–70
  considerations for, 60–61
  finding right fit in, 63–65
  General Counsel and, 74,
    75, 76–77
  introduction to, 57–58
  managing lawyers and,
    70–72
  networking and, 67–68
  obtaining, 58–59
  plan/chance and, 61–63
  selecting/managing outside
    counsel for, 72–74
  specialization for, 74–75
International judge,
  125–135
International law
  career in, 12, 17–19, 33,
    37–39
  defined, 17
  entering field of, 50–52
  environment for, 18
  foreign viewpoint on, 41–45
  introduction to, 33
  lifestyle and, 18–19
  mentors for, 20–21
  non-linear career in, 197–205
  principles of, 129
  private, 42
  public, 12, 42
  solo practitioner and, 49–56
  suggestions for, 43–45
  tips for, 43–45

International Law News, 134
International law practice
  globalization and, 184–185
  introduction to, 183
  launching/growing,
    183–195
International Law Society, 177
International lawyer, 34
International Lawyer, The, 180
International Legal Assistance
  Resource Center
  (ILRC), 158
International Legal Exchange
  (ILEX), 134
International publications, 45
International rule of law
  attorney, 151–160
  becoming, 159–160
  diplomatic work of,
    155–156
  journey in, 151–153
  substantive work of,
    153–155
  technical legal assistant
    providers and, 156–159
International Swaps and
  Derivatives Association
  (ISDA), 5
International trade, experience
  in, 31
International trade law,
  137–149
  balancing family/work and,
    143–145
  dispute settlement and,
    139–140
  equal/better opportunities
    and, 142–143

introduction to, 137–139
litigation and, 139–140
technical assistance and, 142
trade agreements and,
    139–140
trade-related legislation
    and, 140–141
U.S. exporters/investors
    and, 141–142
International treaties, 129
International web sites,
    222–223
International work, 190
Internet. *See also* Web sites
    foreign clients and, 167–169
    impact of, 164–165
    international law and,
        133–134
    small-firm international law
        practice and (*See* Small-
        firm international law
        practice)
Internet resources, 221–223
InternetBar.org, 163
Internships, 121–122, 134
Interpersonal skills, small-firm
    international law practice
    and, 171
Interview, 90, 186
Interview skills, 187
In-the-money, 10
Intimidation, in Kosovo, 129,
    130–131
Intranets, 170
Investigations, ICTY and,
    115–116
Investors, international trade
    law and, 141–142

Iran-U.S. Claims Tribunal, 96,
    97, 105
Iraq, 142
Iraqi Special Tribunal, 112
ISDA. *See* International Swaps
    and Derivatives
    Association (ISDA)

J

Jackson, John, 55
JAG. *See* Judge Advocate
    General (JAG)
Jessen, Pamela, 137
Job choices, compromises
    in, 20
Johnson, Lyndon, 50
*Journal of International
    Arbitration*, 98, 107
*Journal of International Law
    and Commerce*, 12
Judge Advocate General
    (JAG), 17
Judicial reform, international
    rule of law attorney
    and, 154
Juripax, 165
Justice Department, 141. *See
    also* U.S. Department of
    Justice
Justice Reform Practice
    Group, 158

K

Kaman, Marilyn J., 125
Kazakhstan, 153
Kempe, Dianna, 55
Kenya, 165
Keraterm prison camp, 111

Khmer Rouge, 112, 122, 133
King, Henry, 55
Kluwer Law Publishing, 107
Koh, Dean Harold, 55
Kosovo
  background of, 127–128
  international judge in, 125–135
  United Nations Mission in,
    127–131
Kosovo Code of Minor
    Offenses, 129
Kosovo Criminal Code, 129
Kozolchyk, Boris, 55

L

Labor law, 14
Language training, 122–123
Language(s), 23–24, 31, 44, 59,
    60, 66, 120, 122
Large firms. *See* Big/large firms
Latin America, 33, 36–37, 38,
    43, 55, 58, 156
Latin-American transactional
    lawyer, 33–40
Latvia, 153
Law firm practice,
    international law and,
    34–36
Law school, international
    criminal law and, 119
Law(s)
  civil, 100
  commercial, 14
  comparative, 139
  corporate, 14, 31, 171
  cyber, 165
  global cyber, 164, 171
  intellectual property, 171

international (*See*
    International law)
international criminal (*See*
    International criminal law)
international
    humanitarian, 119
international in-house legal
    career and, 69
international trade (*See*
    International trade law)
labor, 14
privacy, 171
private international, 42
public international, 12,
    42, 112
tax, 171
trade, 139
U.S. securities/banking, 171
Lawyer(s)
  cyber, 166–167
  disabled, 143
  ICTY and, 113–116
  international, 34
  international derivatives, 3–10
Latin-American transactional,
    33–40
  managing, 70–72
  minority, 143
  transactional, 33–40
  women, 142–143
Lawyers Committee for Human
    Rights, 123
LCIA, 107, 108
Leave benefits, 145
Lebanon, 134
Leeson, Nick, 8
Legal advisory section, ICTY
    and, 116

Legal career web sites, 223
Legal education reform,
    international rule of law
    attorney and, 155
Legal profession reform,
    international rule of law
    attorney and, 154
Legal Services Corporation, 30
Leigh, Monroe, 55
Lewis, Eleanor Roberts,
    55, 137
Liberia, 134
Lieberthal, Kenneth, 87, 89
Lifestyle
    admirality practice and, 83
    international law and,
        18–19
    international trade law and,
        138, 144
Living abroad, international
    criminal law and, 120
London, 4, 5, 6, 55, 81, 82
London Court of International
    Arbitration, 99
Low, Lucinda, 55
Loyalty, 15

M

*Made in the USA Foundation v.
    U.S.*, 141
Management Sciences for
    Development, Inc., 157
Management Systems
    International, 157
Manager, 72
Marceau, Marcel, 32
Maritime Law Association of
    the United States (MLA), 83

Markus, Andrew J., 33
Márquez, Gabriel García, 25
Martindale-Hubbell, 83
Massachusetts, 141
Maternity leave, in France, 19
Mayre Rasmussen award, 55
McDonald, Gabrielle
    Kirk, 118
MCOL. *See* Money Claim Online
    (MCOL)
*Mealey's International
    Arbitration Report*, 98,
    102, 107
Mears, Rona, 55
Mediation/arbitration
    suites, 170
Medical benefits, 145
Medium-size firms, 36
Men, career and, 19
Mentors, 20–21, 24, 72, 76,
    91, 106
Merchant Marine, 83
Mexico, 173
Meyers-Briggs, 187
Micronesia, 174
Middle East, 7, 13, 15, 16, 55,
    156, 187
Millennium Goals, 171
Millennium/IP3 Partners,
    LLC, 157
Milosevic, Slobodan, 127
Ministry of Commerce, 93
Minority lawyers,
    international
    trade law and, 143
Mitigation, international
    rule of law attorney
    and, 155

MLA. *See* Maritime Law Association of the United States (MLA)
Money Claim Online (MCOL), 166
Money laundering, 113
Moore, Janet H., 183, 193
Moreno, Mario, 32
Moscow Conference, 201, 202
Morley, David, 184
Moyer, Homer E., Jr., 197
Mullerat, Ramon, 55
Mundis, Daryl A., 111
Murder, 128
Murphy, Betty Southard, 55

N

NAEYC. *See* National Association for the Education of Young Children (NAEYC)
NAFTA. *See* North American Free Trade Agreement (NAFTA)
National Association for the Education of Young Children (NAEYC), 144
National Center for State Courts, 158
National Foreign Trade Council, Crosby v., 141
National origin, 56
NATO, 128
Navy, 83, 118, 198
Nebraska Supreme Court, 173
Negotiations, experience in, 31
Net, 10
Netherlands, 16, 120

Netting, 9–10
Network/networking
China and, 93–94
choices for, 173–181
five-point checklist for, 174–181
international criminal law and, 123
international derivatives lawyer and, 24
international in-house legal career and, 67–68, 71
international law career and, 134–135
international law practice and, 53, 54
Internet and, 170
introduction to, 173–174
launching/growing international law practice and, 186, 188–189, 194
Never Eat Alone, 194
New York, 4, 36–37, 54, 81, 82, 83, 96–97, 117, 176, 198
New York Times, The, 180
New Zealand, 80
NGO. *See* Nongovernmental organization (NGO)
Nongovernmental organization (NGO), 17, 30, 31, 92, 123
Non-linear career, 197–205
North Africa, 156
North America, 50, 107
North American Free Trade Agreement (NAFTA), 139–140, 141
Nuremberg trials, 112

O

O'Connor, Sandra Day, 55, 202
OECD Convention on Bribery.
    See Organization for
    Economic Cooperation
    and Development
    (OECD) Convention on
    Bribery
Office of Legal Aid, ICTY
    and, 114
Office of Public Information
    Services, ICTY and, 114
Office of the High
    Representative, 134
Office of the Legal Advisor, 105
Office of the Prosecutor (OTP),
    113, 115–116, 118
Office of the United States
    Trade Representative
    (USTR), 92, 146–147
*One Hundred Years of
    Solitude*, 25
One-liners, 9–10
Online conferencing tools, 170
Online relationships, 167
Online services, small-firm
    international law practice
    and, 165–166
OPIC. *See* Overseas Private
    Investment Corporation
    (OPIC)
Organization for Economic
    Cooperation and
    Development (OECD)
    Convention on Bribery, 139
Organized crime, 128
Orwell, George, 26
OTC. *See* Over-the-counter

OTP. *See* Office of the
    Prosecutor (OTP)
Out-of-the-money, 10
Outside counsel, selecting/
    managing, 72–74
Overseas Private Investment
    Corporation (OPIC), 147
Over-the-counter, 7, 9, 10

P

PACT, Inc., 158
PADCO, 158
Palau, 174
Paralegal, 13
Parental leaves of absence, in
    France, 19
Paris, 11, 12, 13, 21, 52–53, 106
Parliamentarians, international
    rule of law attorney
    and, 154
Pathways programs, 88, 90
Peace Corps, 28, 29, 151
Peat Marwick, 13
Pennsylvania, 12
PepsiCo, Inc., 51–52
Pepys, Mary Noel, 151
Persian Gulf, 82
Personal brand, 192–194
Pfund, Peter, 55
Philadelphia, 11
Planning and Development
    Collaborative
    International, 158
Podcasts, 167, 170, 193
Poland, 139
Postconflict mitigation,
    international rule of law
    attorney and, 155

PowerPoint, 167

Practical Career Advice for Young International Attorneys: How to Build a Killer Resume, Network Effectively, Create Your Own Opportunities, and Live Happily Ever After, 174

Practice's International Commercial Arbitration Committee, 98

"Practitioner's Workshop," 200–201

Price Waterhouse, 14

Prijedor, 111

Primary crossover, 170

Priorities, 19, 63, 66, 67

Prioritization, 66

Privacy laws, 171

Private contracts, 7

Private international law, 42

Privatization, international rule of law attorney and, 153

Pro bono work, 153, 202

Professional associations, 177–178

Professor, 17

Promotion, 74–75

Proofreading, 181

Prosecutions, ICTY and, 115

Public integrity, international rule of law attorney and, 155

Public international law, 12, 42, 112

Publications, international, 45

Q

Questions, 22, 63–64

R

Race, 56

Racial diversity, 83

Rainmaking, 191

Rasmussen, Mayre, 55

Really Simple Syndication (RSS), 170

Reform, 154–155, 159

Regional Police Headquarters, 131

Registry, ICTY and, 113, 114

Relationship(s)
  e-mail, 66
  for international in-house legal career, 65–67, 68, 74
  international law and, 38
  online, 167
  telephone, 66

Relatives, hiring, 72–73

Religious diversity, 83

Reputations, 101, 192–194

Research, 63

Research Triangle Institute, 158

Resilience, 135

Résumé, 174–177, 179, 181

Rholl, Edward, 163

RICO statute, 121

Risk
  credit, 10
  international in-house legal career and, 69–70

ROLI. *See* ABA Rule of Law Initiative (ROLI)

Rotterdam, 16

RSS. *See* Really Simple
Syndication (RSS)
Rules of Procedure and
Evidence, ICTY and, 117
Russia, 8, 142

S

Salomon Brothers, 4, 5
San Francisco, 83
Sartre, Jean-Paul, 28
Saudi Arabia, 66
Schering-Plough, 85
Schildhaus, Aaron, 49
Securities, derivatives as, 7
Securities/banking laws, 171
Security Council, ICTY and, 113
Self-assessment, 186–187
Senie, Allyson L., 137
Senior Executive Service
(SES), 143
Serbian Criminal Code of
1989, 129
SES. *See* Senior Executive
Service (SES)
Sexual preferences, 56
Shihata, Ibrahim, 55
Shipping, 81. *See also*
Admirality practice
Shutter Stock, 165
Sick leave, 145
Sierra Leone, 134
Sikirica, Duško, 111, 118
Singapore, 65, 80, 82
Singapore International
Arbitration Center, 108
Slovakia, 153
Small firms, 35, 37

Small-firm international law
practice, 163–172
foreign clients and, 167–169
global legal environment
and, 164–167
introduction to, 163–164
Smuggling, 128
*So You Want to Be a
Lawyer*, 34
Sociology Theory, 188
Sohn, Louis, 55
Solo practitioner, international
law and, 49–56
Sommerfield Communications,
Inc., 193
Sommerfield, Frank, 193
South Africa, 80, 142
South America, 82
Soviet Union, 118, 152, 201
S&P 500, 8
Spain, 66
Speakers, 178–179
Special Court for Sierra Leone,
112, 122
Specialization, for international
in-house legal career, 74–75
Spoken communication
skills, 121
Staff, international in-house
legal career and, 71
Starbucks, 165
State Department, 92, 147, 201.
See also U.S. Department
of State
Steward, David, 55
Stockholm Chamber of
Commerce, 108

Study abroad, international criminal law and, 120
Studying abroad, 207–219
Style, international in-house legal career, 69
Substantive work, of international rule of law attorney, 153–155
Swartz, Salli A., 11, 163
Switzerland, 173
Symantec Corporation, 59

T
Tax laws, 171
Tax Lawyer, The, 89
Team
  in international criminal law, 121
  for international in-house legal career, 69, 70, 71, 72
Technical legal assistant providers, 156–159
Telephone communication, 168
Telephone relationships, 66
Terrorism, 113, 128
Think tanks, 92
Time
  admirality practice and, 83
  international law and, 19
Titanic, 81
Tito, Josef, 127
Tokyo, 82, 83
Tokyo trials, 112
Tolerance, 56
Torts Branch, 83

Trade agreements, in international trade law, 139–140
Trade groups, 192
Trade, international, 31
Trade law, 139
Training
  for admirality practice, 83
  language, 122–123
Transactional lawyer, 33–40
Transnational corporation, 30
Traveling, 23–24
Treaty of Rome, 113
Trends, international in-house legal career, 69
Tunheim, Jack, 125
Tunisia, 139

U
Ukraine, 153
UN Commission on International Trade Law (UNCITRAL), 106
UN International Institutions Committee, 134
UNDP. *See* United Nations Development Programme (UNDP)
United Kingdom, 6, 23, 50, 98, 107, 120, 165, 166
United Nations, 17, 29, 86, 111, 122, 127–131, 134, 135
United Nations Development Programme (UNDP), 158–159
United Nations Mission in Kosovo (UNMIK), 127–128

United States Agency for International Development (USAID), 147, 157–158

United States, résumés in, 174

United Steelworkers v. U.S., 141

UNMIK. *See* United Nations Mission in Kosovo (UNMIK)

Urban Institute, 158

U.S. Agency for International Development (USAID), 157

U.S. Court of Appeals for the Federal Circuit, 180

U.S. Court of International Trade, 173–174, 180

U.S. Customs and Border Protection, 147

U.S. Department of Commerce, 92, 94, 137, 138. *See also* Commerce Department

U.S. Department of Housing and Urban Development (HUD), 138

U.S. Department of Justice, 80, 83. *See also* Justice Department

U.S. Department of State, 105–106, 185. *See also* State Department

U.S., Made in the USA Foundation v., 141

U.S. securities/banking laws, 171

U.S. Trade Representative's Office, 140, 141

U.S., United Steelworkers v., 141

USAID. *See* United States Agency for International Development

U.S.-Australia Free Trade Agreement, 139

U.S.-Japan Automotive Agreement, 139

USTR. *See* Office of the United States Trade Representative (USTR)

V

Vacation, in France, 19

Venugopal, K. K., 55

Verbal communication, 24

Versatility, 184–185

Vienna, 106

Virtual bar association, 163

Volunteering/volunteerism, 92, 106–107

W

Wall Street, 3–4

Wallace, Don, 55

War crimes, 113, 128, 133

War Crimes Chapter, 134

Washington, D.C., 30, 50, 53–54, 83, 176, 198

Web 2.0 social/business net working sites, 170

Web site templates, 170

Web sites. *See also* Internet for Blue Nile, 165 for The Claim Room, 165 court, 133–134 federal government, 146–148, 221–222 Hieros Gamos, 188 international, 222–223

Web sites *(cont.)*
  for international
    commercial arbitration,
      99, 107
  for internships in
    international criminal
    law, 122
  for Juripax, 165
  legal career, 223
  for MCOL, 166
  MLA, 83
  for Shutter Stock, 165
  small-firm international
    law practice and,
    165, 167
  UN employment, 122
Webcasts, 170
Wedgwood, Ruth, 55
WHO, 17
Wikis, 170
WIPO. *See* World Intellectual
  Property Organization
  (WIPO)
Wojcik, Mark E., 173, 174
Women
  admirality practice and, 83
  career and, 19
  in international law, 55
  international rule of law
  attorney and, 155
  international trade law and,
    138, 142–143
  mentors and, 21
  work-family balance and, 65
Women lawyers, 142–143

Work, 62, 143–145
  diplomatic, 155–156
  international, 190
    of international rule of
    law attorney, 154
  substantive, 153–155
Work spaces, small-firm
  international law practice
  and, 170
Work-family balance, 65
World Affairs Council, 192
World Bank, The, 58–59, 158
World Intellectual Property
  Organization (WIPO),
    17, 106, 107, 108
*World Is Flat: A Brief History
  of the 21st Century,
  The*, 184
World Trade Organization
  (WTO), 139, 140, 141, 201
Wright, Janet, 57–77
Written communication
  skills, 121
WTO. *See* World Trade
  Organization (WTO)

Y

*Yearbook of the International
  Council on Commercial
  Arbitration (ICCA)*, 99
Yugoslavia, 111, 112, 117

Z

Zimmerman, Jim, 93